The Ultimate Chili Cookbook

History, Geography, Fact, and Folklore of Chili

W.C. Jameson

Republic of Texas Press

Library of Congress Cataloging-in-Publication Data

Jameson, W.C., 1942 - .
  The ultimate chili cookbook : history, geography, fact, and
folklore of chili / W.C. Jameson.
      p. cm.
  ISBN 1-55622-652-7 (pbk.)
  1. Chili con carne. I. Title.
TX749.J36   1999
641.8'23—dc21   98-53208
                                    CIP

Republic of Texas Press is an imprint of Wordware Publishing, Inc.

Printed in the United States of America

ISBN 1-55622-652-7
10 9 8 7 6 5 4 3 2
9901

All inquiries for volume purchases of this book should be addressed to Wordware Publishing, Inc., at 2320 Los Rios
Boulevard, Plano, Texas 75074. Telephone inquiries may be made by calling:
(972) 423-0090

Contents

Chapter

Other books by W.C. Jameson:

Bubba Speak: Texas Folk Sayings
Exploring Branson: A Family Guide
Return of Assassin John Wilkes Booth
Return of the Outlaw Billy the Kid
Return of the Outlaw Butch Cassidy
Tales of the Guadalupe Mountains
Unsolved Mysteries of the Old West

Chapter 1

Introduction

*C*hili con carne can be, and often is, many different things to different people.

To some it is merely a dish, nothing more than a bowl of spicy food. To others it is a topping for hot dogs. But the true chili faithful have no time or temperament for such things. Serious chili cooks and chili eaters—and their numbers are legion and growing—regard chili as so much more than mere food.

Among the purists, the preparation and eating of chili has been elevated to an art form. Nutritionists are now giving chili a second look and finding some good things to say. Many others consider cooking and eating chili a form of recreation, some regard it as a kind of therapy, a few liken it to a branch of medicine, and many perceive it as a form of entertainment. To growing numbers of chilimeisters, cooking chili represents an opportunity for competition and provides a level of culinary excitement. Still others are convinced chili is an aphrodisiac, and some even maintain chili is a spiritual experience.

Whatever one's orientation or preference as it relates to chili, this special dish, in its many forms and in so many ways, has become part and parcel of the culture of North America, some would even say the world.

Margaret Cousins, the venerable editor at Doubleday books, once stated, "Chili is not so much a food as a state of mind." Harry James, the famous band

leader, trumpet player, and a man who surely knew his chili, once said, "Next to jazz music, nothing lifts the spirit and strengthens the soul more than a good bowl of chili." Francis X. Tolbert, a Texan long associated with chili, once wrote, "A bowl of chili is a haunting, mystic thing."

The late, great humorist Will Rogers loved chili and spoke of it often. Rogers rated the quality of life in towns around the United States on the basis of the chili found at each one. His survey was kind of a forerunner to today's popular places rated surveys. Rogers' only criterion was, of course, chili. According to Rogers, Coleman, Texas, was at the top of his list.

To the devoted, a good bowl of chili is all of the above and more. Well-prepared, authentic chili, according to the believers, transcends all these things and becomes, in truth, as offered by Cousins, a state of mind.

Good chili is a noble thing, something that can bring pleasure, nirvana, and peace of mind. Bad chili, on the other hand, can be a horrible experience.

Food historians are in complete agreement that chili had its origins in Texas. During its formative years and early evolution, chili was beef (chopped or cubed), peppers (anchos or pequins, pulped or crushed), garlic (minced or chopped), cumin, oregano, and salt, all cooked together and allowed to simmer for at least a couple of hours. Many purists around today still cook their chili according to this tried and true recipe, seldom varying from it.

As the inevitable craving for chili eventually began spreading throughout the country during the late 1800s, other regional cultures modified it on the basis of available ingredients, taste preferences, and sometimes from just messing around with the basic recipe. Some have found adding certain ingredients to their liking, such things as onions, tomato, cayenne, thyme, beer, and broth. Still others have gone to what many traditionalists consider extremes by adding

other such nontraditional ingredients as celery, beans, spaghetti, bell peppers, tequila, whiskey, and sugar. Those who like thick chili add flour, masa harina, or cracker meal. Devotees of thinner chili add various kinds of liquids ranging from water to liquor.

As a food, chili, if prepared correctly, can be good for you. Trimmed of fat and cooked in olive oil, the meat provides necessary protein. The peppers used in chili are rich in vitamins A and C and, according to historical and contemporary folklore and practice, have been used to treat a number of conditions including toothache, gout, colic, ague, seasickness, colds, sore throat, and dropsy. Chile peppers have been known to aid digestion and clarify the blood. According to physicians, a regular diet of chiles helps rid the body of fats, lowers cholesterol levels, and reduces the possibility of heart attack. Several studies have shown us that regular consumers of chile peppers, such as Southwestern Indians and Mexicans, generally experience a lower incidence of heart disease than do most Americans.

Chili may be the most misunderstood food in America, if not the entire world. Many believe chili is a Mexican food, a notion fostered by references to such in movies and cartoons. This is, however, a false notion. Chili, though made with some ingredients from Meso-America, is a uniquely American dish.

Many are convinced chili must always be fiery hot. It can be, and often is, but doesn't have to be. Over time, chili cooks learn to adjust amounts of seasonings based on preference and tolerance.

Arguments have been waged and fistfights fought over whether or not to add beans to chili, a debate that rages to this day. Additionally, there even remains some confusion and disagreement over the appropriateness of adding tomato to chili.

Chili was once banned by fundamentalist churches. Back in the 1890s, chili was a relatively new dish and generally unknown outside of Texas. During the latter part of that decade, Myers' Cafe opened up in the small town of McKinney, located a few miles north of Dallas, and featured chili. This event caused immediate controversy.

A few McKinney residents were leery of this relatively new and unknown food and claimed it could ruin one's insides. Testimony to that effect was solicited from physicians and passed around as fact.

Parents forbade their children to eat chili, claiming it would stunt their growth, cause disfigurement, and render them idiots. Then, as now, all one had to do to get a youngster to try anything was simply forbid him to do so. In no time at all, the youth of McKinney were spending their allowances on bowls of chili down at Myers' Cafe. At all hours of the day, the tiny eatery was filled with kids from twelve to sixteen years of age gobbling up chili at twelve cents a bowl.

This kind of disobedience could not go unpunished. Letters began appearing in the McKinney newspaper that spoke of the loose morals of the town's youth. Food was for sustenance, claimed one of the letter writers, not for enjoyment, and for a child to take so much pleasure from a simple bowl of food was an evil thing that could lead one down the road to greater sins.

It didn't take long for McKinney's fundamentalist churches to get into the act. Ever on the lookout for something to ban, many of the town's preachers were condemning chili from the pulpit and preaching sermons about "sinful indulgence in a food that was prepared by Satan himself." In fact, for a long time in McKinney, chili was called the "Soup of the Devil."

All of this anti-chili screaming and hollering did little more than get normal people more and more interested in and curious about this new and forbidden dish. As a result, it was standing room only at Myers' Cafe from morning until

night, seven days a week, as McKinney citizens lined up for a taste of this youth-corrupting food. It was also reported that one or two of the town's fundamentalist preachers were actually seen slurping up some of this Soup of the Devil. Eventually, cooler heads prevailed, common sense intruded, and "the great chili furor," as it was called by newspaper columnist Francis X. Tolbert, died down.

Chili remains controversial and misunderstood to this day for other reasons as well. In fact, there even exists throughout the country a great deal of confusion on how to spell "chili."

According to chili scholars, the origin of the word comes from Aztec Indians who thrived in Mexico around the time Columbus visited some of the Caribbean islands. Over time, the word "chili" has become the only acceptable term, socially and otherwise, for the bowl of meat, peppers, and seasoning we know and love today, the traditional "bowl o' red." On examining the existing literature, as well as dozens of restaurant menus across the United States, one encounters multiple variations on the spelling of the word "chili."

Sometimes the word "chile" is found. In truth, chile, with an "e" at the end instead of an "i," refers to peppers from the *capsaicin* family. "Chile" is synonymous with chile pepper, whether red or green. Chile peppers, of course, are a principle ingredient in chili.

The American South seems to offer the greatest variation in the spelling of "chili." South of the Mason-Dixon Line we have encountered "chille," "chilli," "chilie," "chillie," and even "chililie." In the Midwest we found "chilly" and "chilley."

Once, while stopping for dinner at a roadside cafe in Iowa, we saw a menu listing for something called "chilly con carny."

Chili purists recommend never eating chili at places where it is not spelled correctly.

The Ultimate Chili Cookbook you now hold in your hands represents an offering—a helping, if you will—of the siftings of more than three decades of research on the history, geography, and lore of chili, as well as over 135 recipes, a portion of a collection that has grown over the years.

While the subject of food, and in particular chili, appropriately lends itself to an academic treatment, we have refrained from doing so here. Chili is far too much fun to be dragged through a jungle of tedious jargon and cumbersome footnotes. Chili is to be enjoyed, not endured.

The recipes included in this book are the result of decades of searching, sampling, and experimenting. Some of those offered here are traditional, some were given to me by friends and fellow chilistos, all kindred spirits of chiliana. Many were collected on the road during travels from coast to coast, border to border. A few originally came from old and long out-of-print cookbooks as well as some from the extant literature. All have been modified over the years as a result of experimentation, from adding something here and deleting something there, and from a variety of innovations inflicted on them from time to time.

Additionally, a number of these recipes are of my own design. All have been tried, kitchen tested, modified, and ultimately developed to become what is presented in these pages. Our hope is that you enjoy preparing and dining on these dishes as much as we enjoyed working on them and with them over the years.

One of the glories of cooking and eating chili, in addition to all of those mentioned previously, is that they are never ending processes. No matter how perfect a recipe, the experimentation continues and the search goes on. Such culinary exploration and discovery remains a worthwhile, indeed, a noble goal, and one which we shall pursue until the last pepper is sliced.

Chapter II

The History of Chili

Wish I had time for just one more bowl of chili.
Alleged last words of Kit Carson

Researching the history of chili con carne has proven to be a rewarding yet in many ways a troublesome undertaking. The researcher encounters a multitude of earlier efforts, many of which yield a number of different claims for origins. As with most history, the difficulties arise in trying to separate fact from fiction and, in some cases, fact from legend.

As it turns out, the serious chili researcher winds up being confronted with dozens of theories relating to the origin of this precious brew. Strong claims for any one of the theories can, and have, resulted in disagreements ranging from relatively quiet intellectual discussions to brawls. Each of the claimants, or groups of claimants, it appears, remains steadfastly loyal to his own particular theory and is not likely to be swayed by the opinions of others. Nor do they seem to be the least bit influenced by historical facts.

Ultimately, regardless of the specific theory of origin one adheres too, it appears quite unlikely that anyone will ever discover who actually made the first pot of chili. Chili, as we know it and love it today, like many other things,

probably evolved over time and involved the contribution of a number of different cultures and individuals.

During the early settlement phases of the Texas Southwest, many literate explorers, soldiers, and others passed through the region: the French explorer Pages in 1767; Zebulon Pike in 1807; Benjamin Lundy in 1833; the German scientist Roemer in 1846; the intrepid Frederic Law Olmsted in 1854. Although E. DeGolyer, the millionaire and scholarly chilisto, once wrote that this unique dish was likely started during the 1840s, not a single one of the aforementioned observant and curious individuals who traveled Texas and the Southwest ever mentioned chili in their journals and reports. If chili had existed in the regions traveled and explored, it surely would have been noted.

In 1862 it was reported that Confederate soldiers assigned to San Antonio grew boisterous in the city's plaza and wrecked a number of food stands. While several different kinds of food were mentioned, such as tamales and stews for example, there was not a single mention of chili.

Around the same time, a visitor to San Antonio named Sidney Lanier wrote in detail of the wonders and delights of the city, but there was no mention of chili in his pages.

In 1874 *Scribner's* magazine published an article about San Antonio by Edward King. King wrote about a number of things, including the food he encountered there, but chili was not among them.

Joe Cooper once wrote about a painting by Thomas Allen, an artist who spent some time in San Antonio in 1879. Cooper notes that in one of Allen's paintings of the plaza, something that looks suspiciously like a chili stand is represented.

During a visit through Texas during the early 1880s, two authors named Knox and Sweet wrote rather critically about Mexican and Southwestern food, but there was still no mention of chili.

In 1882 *Gould's Guide to San Antonio* mentions "chili con carne" and its availability at various locations around the plaza. This, as far as we can determine, is the first mention of chili in print.

Somebody named Frank H. Buschick wrote a book that included an entire chapter on San Antonio's chili queens who, he says, were in full operation during 1895.

In 1896 William Gebhardt began mixing the spices used in the making of chili and selling packets of them throughout San Antonio and surrounding environs. Demand soon grew for his now famous chili powder, and by 1899 it was a full-fledged manufacturing and sales operation in the Alamo City.

In 1897 chili was mentioned again in print, this time in a novel entitled *Wolfville* and authored by somebody named Alfred Henry Lewis.

In 1899, according to Cooper, a Mexican food restaurant was opened in San Antonio that served, among other items, chili. The principal clientele, says Cooper, who in turn quoted Buschick, were Americans. According to San Antonio lore, this is supposed to be the first Mexican food restaurant in the United States, though others have had similar claims made for them.

The above chronology pins down the origins of chili, more or less, to sometime between 1879 and 1882. This not an inarguable position, merely one arrived at based on some few available facts.

With the time period out of the way, we can now turn our attention to some prevailing theories relative to the origins of chili. Each of those presented below has it proponents and opponents, and we make no claim for the superiority of

one over the other. They are presented, as best we can manage, in chronological order.

The New World Theory

Peppers, such as those used in the preparation of chili, are native to that geographic region scholars have taken to calling Meso-America, a vast region consisting of Mexico, Central America, and most of northern South America. The area was home to Aztecs, Mayas, Incas, and other tribes.

It is well known that the natives of this region regularly dined on chile peppers mixed with meat and herbs, and they apparently did so for centuries prior to the arrival of the Spanish explorers. This dish, which clearly resembled chili as we know it today, was a staple of the Meso-Americans who, in turn, introduced it to the visiting Spaniards. The Spaniards, unfamiliar with the capsicum vegetable called chile, confused them with the more familiar bell peppers. Mistakenly, they simply named the chiles peppers, a name which has stuck over the ages.

Regardless of what the Europeans called chiles, they certainly took a liking to this somewhat spicy food, and as they continued their explorations and invasions throughout Meso-America and northward into what is now the United States, they likely carried the ingredients and cooking techniques along with them and probably even added a few of their own contributions to the plate.

The Lady in Blue Theory

One claim for the early existence of what seems to be chili or something closely resembling it, does, in fact, come from a legend, specifically an old American Indian tale. A number of Southwestern tribes tell of being visited by a mysterious woman dressed entirely in blue. On these visits, the stranger introduced the indigenes to Christianity and instructed the people to prepare a

glorious welcome for the eventual coming of the Spanish missionaries.

When the Spaniards finally arrived, they were a bit mystified by all the stories about the lady in blue, whom they called *La Dama de Azul*. Missionary priest Alonso de Benarifes and Spanish King Philip IV believed the lady in blue to be the spirit of Sister Mary of Agreda, a nun who lived in a convent in Castile, Spain.

The story goes that Mary entered the convent in 1618 when she was sixteen years of age. Not long afterward, she fell into a series of trances, some of which lasted for several days. When she finally recovered from these trances, she told of visiting a distant land where she walked among the natives and spoke to them about Christianity. With amazing accuracy, Sister Mary of Agreda described the landscape and inhabitants of the American Southwest and provided information about their language and food ways. One particular dish she recorded consisted of venison, onions, tomatoes, and chile peppers, the earliest known recipe for what could easily be taken for, or mistaken for, chili.

The Canary Islander Theory

The Canary Islands are a Spanish possession located in the Atlantic Ocean a couple hundred miles off the northwest coast of Africa. This popular theory holds that chili was first concocted by immigrant Canary Islanders who arrived in San Antonio during the early 1700s. Canary Island cuisine was often characterized by the use of curry, but finding little or none of that seasoning in San Antonio, the newcomers availed themselves of locally produced chile peppers as well as other herbs and seasonings, and eventually created a prototype of chili. This dish, no doubt, resembled something they ate back home. The Canary Islander theory claims a surprisingly high number of proponents and seems to be one of the most often quoted in the available literature.

The Cultural Mix Theory

Another theory holds that chili may have been a dish that evolved simply as a result of the mixing of a variety of cultures that settled in San Antonio during the early- to mid-1700s. Among these were the aforementioned Canary Islanders who were joined by Mexicans, a few French, and even some Italians and American Indians. As a result of the subsequent interaction, mixing, sharing, and borrowing, the dish called chili resulted, likely out of expediency.

Missionary Theory

Some believe chili had its origins during the time of the religious conversion of Indians in the American Southwest. According to writers Susan Hazen-Hammond and Eduardo Fuss, a Jesuit priest observed the natives preparing a stew consisting of chile peppers and meat all cooked together in lard. Hazen-Hammond and Fuss even included a recipe for this early chili in their book *Chile Pepper Fever: Mine's Hotter Than Yours*.

No one doubts the observations of the Jesuit priest, however it is also quite likely that the Indians had been preparing and eating this stew centuries before the missionaries ever showed up.

Author and chilisto Joe Cooper offers a somewhat different point of view. He suggests that the Jesuit priests themselves may have actually arrived at the recipe for chili as a means of stretching the meager food supplies, a situation that often existed at the early missions.

The Texas Army Theory

Dogged researcher Joe Cooper also found reference to a chili-like dish that had been assembled to feed the Texas army in 1835. According to Cooper, when military officials were mobilizing recruits in San Antonio, they found it necessary to feed large numbers of people. Mexican cooks were hired to prepare what was available, which turned out to be a hearty stew concocted from

beef cooked with red pepper, a kind of prototypical chili.

The Gold Rush Theory

Some historians insist the origin of chili came at a much later date, specifically around the time of the California Gold Rush. Based on rather scanty evidence provided by a man named E. DeGolyer, this theory suggests that during 1850, a party of Texans, in searching for an easy-to-prepare food they could quickly cook along the trail on their way to the gold fields, came up with a mixture of beef, salt, pepper, and chile peppers, all dried and carried in a tow sack. When it was time for dinner, they simply broke off a piece of the mixture into a pot of boiling water and cooked it until it was ready to eat. If true, this could have been the first chili mix!

The Poor People Theory

Around the 1850s, according to authors Maury Maverick Jr. and Charles Ramsdell, poor people in San Antonio invented chili. Maverick stated that poor folks purchased inferior cuts of meat at low prices, cut them up into bite-sized pieces, and cooked them with chile peppers and onions for flavor.

The Texas Prison Theory

This explanation for the genesis of chili also has its origins in Texas during the mid-1800s. In an effort to provide relatively nutritious meals at a low cost to criminals incarcerated in the state's prisons, somebody came up with a stew consisting of cheap and tough beef mixed with chile peppers and a few spices. This stew, i.e. chili, was reportedly so good that released and paroled prisoners, unable to obtain similar fare in the free world, supposedly committed crimes so they would be returned to prison and jailhouse chili.

The Texas Cowboy Theory

One of the most enduring theories, this explanation also seems to be one of the most often quoted among a lot of chili historians, particularly those from Texas. Cowhands, who were out rounding up cattle and driving them up the various trails to the railheads in Kansas, Nebraska, and other points north during the 1860s and 1870s, were in need of a filling, stick-to-the-ribs type of fare to sustain them on their journey. Cooks often fixed stew on the trail simply because it was easy to do. The meal was prepared from cuts of beef accompanied by onions, herbs, and various seasonings. As one version of this theory goes, some cook presumably ran out of black pepper for seasoning and allegedly added crushed red pepper made from chiles found growing along the way.

The San Antonio Chili Queen Theory

Regardless of how chili originated and evolved, by the 1880s and 1890s it was fairly well established throughout much of Texas and other parts of the American West.

During the 1880s, a ubiquitous feature of some Texas cities, San Antonio in particular, was the presence of sidewalk chili vendors. The vendors, who were mostly women, spooned out bowls of hot, steaming chili to hungry customers on the plazas and squares. The chili queens, as they came to be called, went to great lengths to decorate their booths with elaborate designs and eye-catching colors, all designed to lure customers. Some even hired musicians to perform during business hours.

For decades the San Antonio chili queens served bowls o' red to thousands, if not millions, of people, from their booths. Local merchants and workers frequented the chili stands for lunch, and before long these sidewalk chili vendors grew to become a cultural phenomena. Tourists to the Alamo City made a visit to one of the booths a *de rigeur* stop. This popular outdoor dining activity came

to a screeching halt in 1943, however, when the city health officials shut down the chili queens, claiming unsanitary conditions.

However one interprets the history of chili, the clear consensus is that it is unquestionably American in origin. Even more specifically, chili was originally a Texas food. Arguments continue to rage, however, as to exactly where in Texas this special cuisine had its beginnings. According to a vast number of passionate chili researchers, San Antonio was the birthplace of the now world famous bowl o' red.

Another school of thought, one that claims equally passionate adherents, places the origins of this dish in the brush country of South-Central to Southwest Texas during the time of vast cattle ranches where range cooks made do with what they had. The first chili, they claim, may very well have come from the back of a chuck wagon.

While clearly American and Texan in origin, chili wouldn't be chili without some important ingredients borrowed from Meso-America. Meso-America gets credited simply because chiles—anchos and others, fresh, crushed, and powdered—had their origins in that region.

In spite of the overwhelming evidence that chili was birthed in the Lone Star State, many continue to believe it possesses a specific Mexican origin. A lot of people still labor under the misguided assumption that if a dish is spicy hot, then it has got to be from Mexico. This type of folklore is perpetuated via movies, cartoons, comics, and other media. Many of us who pursue chili adventures around the hemisphere have traveled throughout much of Mexico and have yet to find chili as we know it. Friends who are frequent visitors to Mexico, Central America, and South America claim they have never encountered a single bowl of chili there.

Others—travelers who insist on dining at Mexican restaurants that cater to American tourists, have sometimes claimed encounters with chili. There is a

simple explanation for this: Mexicans are aware that many Americans vacation south of the border and, believing chili to be a Mexican food, simply expect to find it during their wanderings. As a result, and because it makes a certain economic sense, the Mexicans simply make it and serve it.

Employing impeccable logic, Cooper once wrote that if chili had come from Mexico, it should still be found there. The truth is, chili is rare in Mexico.

The Role of the Chili Parlor

According to chili scholars, the chili parlor, an institution that is found today in numerous guises and incarnations around the country, first got started in Texas. Back during the 1920s and 1930s, many small town Texas cafes, operating on a tiny budget, often offered chili and little else. These smallish restaurants specializing in chili soon came to be known as chili parlors and became gathering places for local men and boys alike. Old men discussed politics and played dominoes, teenage boys discussed sports and teenage girls, and businessmen found the chili parlors an ideal and inexpensive place for taking a lunch break.

Some early chili parlors sold chili for around twenty-five cents a bowl, and it was generally accompanied by all the crackers one could eat. Chili parlors were likely responsible for introducing at least of couple of generations of diners to this special dish.

As chili and chili parlors grew to become an important part of the Texas culture, they were encountered by numerous visitors from elsewhere, visitors who found they liked this new and exciting dish called chili, even craved it, and who continued to yearn for it on returning to the north and east from whence they came. As a result, the demand for chili began to grow in such unlikely places as Ohio, Illinois, and New York, and the geographic beginnings of an amazing cultural and culinary journey were underway.

Chapter III

The Geography of Chili

Geography is a science that deals with a seemingly endless number of concepts including, among other things, distance, direction, distribution, diffusion, cultures, acculturation, similarities, differences, and relationships. The study of food can be and often is geographical, and chili in particular lends itself well to these kinds of investigations and interpretations. It is through the science of geography, in fact, that we can perhaps better understand the origins and diffusion of chili throughout a wide variety of cultures, many of which have taken this simple yet significant dish and invited it—indeed, embraced it—into their own culture. As a result, chili has been modified by the various cultures, many of which inflicted their own regional tastes, needs, preferences, and tolerances onto the dish. Because of the constant and continuous modification and adjusting of the recipe, chili varies across the United States from culture to culture as much or more than any other food.

As seen from the previous chapter, chili possesses multiple geographic facets relative to its origins. From the Mexican and Central American Indians we

got the chile peppers. Years of the domestication process undertaken by Mayans, Incas, Aztecs, and Quechuas yielded a variety of chiles that were often traded with other tribes to the north and with residents of the islands of the Caribbean. When Columbus returned from the Caribbean to Europe in 1493, he brought with him, among other things, chile peppers. The peppers were embraced by European cooks, and from there they continued spreading clear into Asia and Indonesia where today they have become an important ingredient in many wonderful dishes.

Peppers diffused via trade from Meso-America into Texas and the American Southwest where they quickly became established both as a food item and as an agricultural crop. In recent years, peppers from New Mexico and California have made their way eastward into the Texas chili hearth.

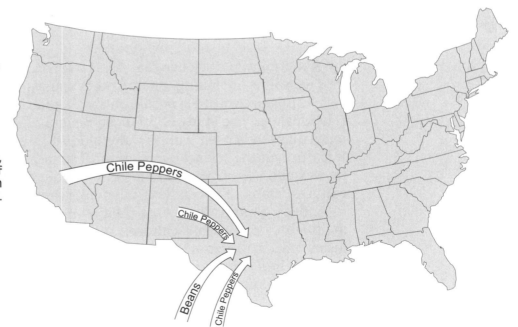

From Meso-America, New Mexico, and California came a variety of ingredients used in the preparation of chili.

Speaking of Meso-America, it should be pointed out here that pinto and other kinds of beans, as well as tomatoes, occasional ingredients in chili, were also domesticated there and eventually diffused throughout the world. The Meso-Americans also gave us chocolate, corn, squash, tobacco, and many other agricultural products.

Continuing with the themes of spatial and cultural differences, it will also be recalled from the previous chapter that during the 1880s the Canary Islanders migrated to San Antonio where, it is believed by many, they were introduced to chile peppers. Finding them quite acceptable and complimentary to many of their dishes, they added them fresh, dried, ground, and in powdered form to their own recipes.

Over the years, chili has certainly evolved, manifesting a variety of incarnations with some of them remarkably different from the type derived during its embryonic years in Texas. The first and still considered by many the purest and most essential recipe contains meat, peppers, garlic, cumin, oregano, and salt. In a relatively short time, this basic guideline has been stretched, padded, modified, ravaged, savaged, and otherwise changed such that chili offers as many variations as do members of the human race.

If chili had any kind of formal introduction to the public in general, it was likely in the streets of San Antonio during the early 1880s. San Antonio was a bustling place in those days with travelers passing through and the growing businesses attracting visitors from states to the north and east. Yankees and others who came to San Antonio quickly became enamored of the chili they found and, on returning to the environs of Ohio, Illinois, New York, and elsewhere, carried with them their appetite for the spicy new dish they enjoyed in Texas. Just as the ingredients and styles that gave rise to chili migrated into Texas, the dish itself was involved in an out-migration. Soon, as a result of the demand, restaurants and cafes in the Midwest and Northeast were featuring

chili on their menus. The farther one got from Texas, the greater the variety of chili was encountered.

Chili diffused from the Texas hearth area to various regions of the United States where it has become a significant part of the culinary culture.

Great Lakes States

The East

The Midwest

California

New Mexico

The South

One man who became instrumental in enhancing the popularity of chili and aiding in its diffusion was the late humorist Will Rogers. While performing on Broadway and elsewhere, Rogers extolled the virtues of chili such that his audience simply had to sample it. Other personalities who followed Rogers, such as the late president of the United States Lyndon B. Johnson, were also instrumental in diffusing chili northward and eastward. Before long, chili was being served in fine restaurants in Chicago and New York, and soon it became quite fashionable among the social elite to dine out on chili from Washington, D.C. to Los Angeles, California.

As chili was gaining a foothold in these far-flung locations miles from the Texas hearth, it continued to undergo changes. Not everyone craved the pepper-generated "heat" so loved by the Texans. In a relatively short time, regional preferences took control and various cultural dictates intruded upon the basic chili recipe. The result was a striking evolution into thousands of different recipes, each possessing certain regional flavors and characteristics.

Southerners, those good folk found, for the most part, below the Mason-Dixon Line and east of the eastern Texas-Oklahoma cross timbers region, enthusiastically embraced chili and wasted no time at all adapting it to their culinary styles. As chili made its way into and throughout the South, some serious modifications occurred. With some few exceptions, Southerners are generally not overly fond of hot, spicy foods. As a result, the basic Texas chili was softened and rounded off by exchanging the harsher chiles for bell peppers, using significantly less chili powder, and adding sugar and beans.

Among collections of chili recipes, the ones from the South more often than not include sugar. This comes as no surprise to food historians—Southern recipes often call for sugar in a variety of dishes, including meat dishes such as stews. Therefore, it wasn't much of a stretch for the Dixielanders to add sugar to chili.

History does not record the first use of beans in chili, but the general consensus is that this practice likely got its start in the American South. Others maintain placing beans in chili may have had its origins in the Midwest, but the South gets the most votes.

Regardless of where the practice originated, it is a well-known fact that beans are found in chili far more often in the East than in the West. Personal experience and consultation with experts who study such things has yielded what geographers call the "Bean Line," a more or less formalized division between the no-beaners of the West and the beaners from the East.

It is believed by numerous chili scholars that the beans were initially added to stretch the chili, or perhaps to serve as a substitute for meat. As time went by, the Southerners not only became accustomed to beans in their chili, they began to really like them. As a result, beans remain a common and even an important ingredient in Southern chili.

The Bean Line. East of the line, beans as an ingredient in chili are far more common than west of the line.

Differences in the meat are also apparent in the South. Here, the traditional coarsely ground or cubed beef gave way to hamburger, most likely as a result of expediency. Beef was never as plentiful in the South as it was in Texas, and the beef that could be obtained was often tough and tasteless. To render the tough beef edible, the residents resorted to grinding it into hamburger.

In the South, bell peppers were, and are, often substituted for chile peppers, the bells generally being more acceptable to the Southern palate than the hotter peppers of the Southwest. Though no one knows for certain, it is also believed by some that tomatoes were first added to chili in the South.

Additionally, the practice of topping a bowl of chili with a dollop of sour cream is often encountered in Southern recipes. This topping, to the surprise of many, is even becoming popular outside of the South and is found throughout parts of the Midwest and East.

One also finds in the South that the meat used in preparing chili is browned and the onions sautéed more often in butter or lard than in olive oil or other types of cooking oil.

The Southern state of Louisiana offers a somewhat spicier chili than most of its Confederate neighbors. Here, the Cajun cooks often add a zesty sausage along with locally grown hot peppers and hot pepper sauces.

Midwestern cultures also offer some interesting variations on the basic chili recipe. In locations such as Illinois, Indiana, and Ohio, chili without beans is seldom found, and the meat always seems to be hamburger. While pinto beans are occasionally encountered, one is more likely to find kidney beans, even lima beans, in their chili. Many purists would regard the addition of lima beans the ultimate blasphemy to a bowl of chili, but it must be remembered that such things are a product of differences in culture.

At the edge of the Midwest, Kansas City, Missouri, has been factored into the nation's chili culture from time to time. Here, chili is often served over a plate of macaroni and called chili-mac, a meal that, oddly, is now found quite often in public school lunchrooms throughout much of the country. Over the years, Kansas City was generally considered a town in which one could often find a decent chili parlor.

Cincinnati is a large and important town in Ohio and in recent years has been calling itself "The Chili Capital of the World." Indeed, some literature received recently states that Cincinnati claims more chili parlors per capita than anyplace else in the United States. The Cincinnati telephone book lists about one hundred chili parlors in this town of some 365,000 souls, about three times the number of McDonald's!

While Texans and other chili purists may not agree or even like it, the fact is that Cincinnati does a booming chili business. The Texans and the purists,

however, would likely not recognize what Cincinnatians call chili, and one principle reason for this is that the version served here was modified by contributions from Greek immigrants.

Recipes gleaned from the fine city of Cincinnati reveal ingredients as nontraditional and diverse as cinnamon, allspice, chocolate, and barbecue sauce. Furthermore, it has become the custom here to pour the chili over a large helping of spaghetti!

The most popular version of chili in Cincinnati, we are told, is called the "Five Way" and consists of a large plate of spaghetti topped with a sauce consisting of hamburger, a number of standard chili seasonings, along with cinnamon, chocolate, allspice, cardamom, tumeric, and barbecue sauce. Heaped atop this is a healthy serving of kidney beans which, in turn, is covered by chopped raw onions. Finally, a sprinkling of grated cheddar cheese is added and allowed to melt. Some Cincinnati chili is even topped with lettuce. The Five Way is customarily served with oyster crackers.

Cincinnatians can also order a Four Way, which comes without onions; a Three Way, which comes without onions and beans (also called a Haywagon); or a Chili Bean, which comes without cheese and onions.

History records that Cincinnati chili was invented by two brothers from Greece who migrated to this Ohio River town and opened a tiny cafe in the early 1920s. Their credentials were related to the fact that they ran a hot dog stand in New York for a couple of years. The brothers, John and Athanas Kiradjieff, experimented with ingredients, eventually coming up with Five Way chili, much, apparently, to the delight of the natives. So popular was the Kiradjieffs' chili, that dozens of other cafes opened during the next few years featuring similar recipes.

Moving northward from the Midwest into the Great Lakes states of Michigan, Minnesota, and Wisconsin, one finds variations of chili that have much in common with their neighbors in Illinois and Indiana. Beans are ubiquitous in Great Lakes states chili—in fact, according to recipes from this area, as well as numerous dining experiences, many of these folks apparently believe that chili is supposed to contain more beans than meat. The beans invariably are canned, and one seems to encounter kidneys more often than any other kind.

Some Wisconsin chilis we've been exposed to in the past contained, instead of kidney beans, such varieties as red beans and lima beans, but never pinto beans. Rather than fresh, dried, or powdered chiles, bottled salsas were often used. Lots of garlic was evident, and the meat was always hamburger.

A handful of recipes filed under the heading "Minnesota Chili" reveal ingredients and techniques for making a hearty chili-like stew, sometimes substituting wild game for hamburger. While some of the recipes resemble others common in the Midwest, a few are quite innovative and include ingredients such as apple cider vinegar or wine. Invariably, beans are plentiful and they are generally kidney.

The industrialized and economically active East is now home to a number of expatriate Texans who drifted into the cooler and most densely populated climes to pursue their fortunes. As a result, the demand for chili remained high, and New York cooks responded by opening a number of chili parlor-style restaurants. While one can find chili in New York that possesses definite Midwestern characteristics, there also happens to be a lot of traditional Texas-style chili. Several chili recipes obtained from a number of New York eateries, which have seen fit to cater to Texas tastes, verify this observation.

One can often find an acceptable bowl of chili in the nation's capital. The tenure of the late President Lyndon B. Johnson in Washington, D.C. led to some

...or popularization of chili in the nation's capital. To this day, one can still find acceptable chili at a number of D.C. establishments, though more often than not it comes with beans, kidneys seemingly more plentiful than any other kind.

Just to the west of Texas in New Mexico, chili is taking on a high-profile identity. Flavorful New Mexico chile peppers—and they are grown in enormous quantities here—contribute some robust and exciting tastes to chili. Pork is commonly added to beef in many of the chilis found in the Land of Enchantment. In some recipes it replaces beef altogether, and the results are delicious. Where beans are used at all, garbanzos have occasionally been employed with good effect. A number of New Mexico recipes call also for a small amount of corn or hominy, each of which offers a flavor that nicely compliments the taste of pork.

Like New Mexico, California is also making a name for itself from the standpoint of chile pepper agriculture, the Anaheims being the most prominent. In spite of this, a lot of California-style chili recipes served up in the big cities use bell peppers instead of chile peppers. Long touted as California's best chili, the recipe found at Chasen's restaurant in Beverly Hills used green bell peppers.

I possess a recipe for something called a California Five Way Chili. The approach is similar to the Cincinnati Five Way in that it involves layering chili, beans, onions, and cheese atop a bed of spaghetti. The principal differences are found in the ingredients in the chili itself. Spicy Mexican chorizo sausage is added to hamburger, and considerably more chili powder is called for. Furthermore, black beans are used instead of kidney beans.

The popularity of chili across the country, indeed, around the world, has naturally led to competition. It is estimated that hundreds of chili cook-offs occur in the United States every year, most of them sanctioned either by the International Chili Society (ICS) or the Chili Appreciation Society International (CASI). Chili cook-offs, like chili itself, have grown to become a cultural institution as well as an art form.

The Chili Appreciation Society International and the International Chili Society oversee much of the chili competition in the United States and elsewhere and are responsible for keeping tabs on chili activity geographically distributed throughout this country and elsewhere. Members of these two organizations come from practically every state in the union. Not only do these fine groups sponsor and sanction cook-offs, they offer an opportunity for kindred spirits and fellow chilimeisters to gather and interact at a variety of locations.

The CASI championship chili cook-off was the reigning chili event in the world between 1967 and 1974, the event being held in the remote West Texas town of Terlingua. As a matter of fact, it still is and continues to attract huge crowds and fierce competition.

Due to differences in philosophy, Carrol Shelby and C.V. Wood broke away from the CASI to form the ICS and established headquarters in Newport Beach, California. One of the first tasks of the new ICS was to establish their own world championship cook-off, which they did and with great success. For years, the ICS world championships were held in California, but in 1996 they moved to Las Vegas, Nevada.

The CASI boasts chili "pods" in about twenty-four of the United States as well as several foreign countries. Each of these pods may hold a local cook-off. Over 400 CASI-sponsored events are held each year and operate according to strict rules. Chili is judged on the basis of aroma, color, taste, aftertaste, and texture. Points are awarded to cooks who place in the top ten at CASI-

...ioned cook-offs, and after receiving a certain critical number, cooks can qualify for the annual national cook-off at Terlingua.

The ICS is a nonprofit organization that sanctions chili cook-offs with specific rules for judging and cooking. Their stated purpose is, in part:

> *. . . to promote, develop, and improve the preparation and appreciation of true chili and to determine each year the World's Champion Chili through officially sanctioned and regulated competitive cook-offs.*

The ICS championship cook-off may likely be the world's largest food contest. During a recent ICS World Championship Chili Cook-Off elimination, over 9,000 cooks from around the country participated. The 250 finalists at Las Vegas competed for $40,000 in prize money, and over 25,000 visitors attended the event.

Both the CASI and the ICS are active in community service and raise money for charities. The CASI has contributed over three quarters of a million dollars to charities over the years. According to the ICS web page, about sixty-five million dollars has been raised by charities holding sanctioned chili cook-offs.

Chili Organizations

Chili Appreciation Society International (CASI)
Web site: http://www.chili.org
To register cook-offs: (800) CASI-HOT (227-4468)
Executive Director (elected to two-year terms)
    Johnye Harriman
    10906 E CR 108
    Midland, TX 79706-5366
    (915) 620-0725 (eve)

International Chili Society (ICS)
Web site: http://www.chilicookoff.com
    International Chili Society
    6755 Speedway Blvd.
    Las Vegas, NV 89115
    (877) 777-4ICS (777-4427) or fax (702) 643-5777

Original Terlingua International Frank X. Tolbert-Wick Fowler Memorial Championship Chili Cook-off
(also known as "Behind the Store" or "Tolbert")
    Viva Terlingua Headquarters
    PO Box 617
    Corsicana, TX 75151-0617
    (903) 874-5601 (phone and fax)

Major Chili Cook-offs

Contact the *Goat Gap Gazette* for current information, PO Box 800, Brookesmith, TX 76827-0800 (915) 646-6914 or fax (915) 646-8564 or goatgap@web-access.net.

January
Amarillo, TX — Make a Wish Chili Cook-off (1st or 2nd weekend)
Contact: Garnier Albus, 4416 S. Fannin St., Amarillo, TX 79110-1711 (806) 353-0500 (eve)

Houston, TX — CyFair Go-Texan Chili & Bar-B-Que Cook-off (2nd Saturday)
Contact: Doris Anderson, 6303 Pecan Wood Dr., Houston, TX 77088-4021 (713) 847-2451 (eve)

February
Yoakum, TX — Land of Leather Chili Cook-off
Contact: Yoakum Chamber of Commerce, PO Box 591, Yoakum, TX 77995 (512) 293-2309

March
Sweetwater, TX — Sweetwater Jaycees Rattlesnake Roundup Chili & BBQ
Cook-off (2nd weekend) Contact: Chamber of Commerce, PO Box 1148, Sweetwater, TX 79556 (915) 235-5488

Cedar Park, TX — 24th San Antonio Pod CASI Cook-off (3rd Saturday)
Contact: Joyce Jowers, 3510 Lakefield, San Antonio, TX 78230 (210) 696-2555 (eve)

April

Jacksonville, FL — Leukemia Society Chili & BBQ Cook-off (1st Saturday)
Contact: Leukemia Society of America, 4019 Woodcock Dr., Ste. 102, Jacksonville, FL 32207
Megan Gardner (904) 398-4845 or (800) 868-0072

Grand Prairie, TX — Prairie Dog Chili Cook-off (1st Sunday)
Contact: Traders Village, 2602 Mayfield Rd., Grand Prairie, TX 75052 (972) 647-2331

Corsicana, TX — Derrick Days Celebration & Frank X. Tolbert Texas State
Cook-off (3rd Saturday) Contact: Al Hopkins, PO Box 617, Corsicana, TX 75151-0617
(903) 874-5601 (phone & fax)

Seguin, TX — CASI Ladies State Chili Championship (3rd Saturday)
Contact: Pat Irving, 208 Galvin, Seguin, TX 78155 (830) 372-4811 days

Houston, TX — Houston Pod Hal John & Judy Wimberly Memorial Cook-off
(4th Saturday) Contact: Al Austin, 6303 Pecan Wood Dr., Houston, TX 77088-4021
(713) 847-2451 (eve)

May

Marble Falls, TX — Howdy Roo Chili Cook-off (1st Saturday)
Contact: Ruby Ross, PO Box 934, Marble Falls, TX 78654 (830) 693-3492

Ennis, TX — Top of Texas Chili Cook-off (3rd Saturday)
Contact: Harvey West, 6966 Dove Creek Dr., Wylie, TX 75098-7750 (972) 442-2677 days

Wichita Falls, TX — Southwest Open Chili Cook-off (Saturday of Memorial Day weekend)
Contact: Jim Ezell, 106 Armada, Wichita Falls, TX 76308-5701 (940) 692-5974

June

Cedar Park, TX — State of Texas Pod Cook-off & Cedar Choppers Festival
(3rd Saturday) Contact: Sue Caffey, 206 CR 434, Rockdale, TX 76567 (512) 446-2364

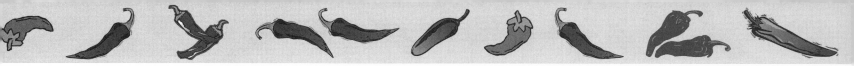

Grand Prairie, TX — Cowtown CASI Chili Cook-off (3rd Saturday)
Contact: Doris Coats, 1645 Priscilla Lane, Irving, TX 75061-2022 (972) 254-5920 (eve)

August
Lewisville, TX — Texas Open Chili Cook-off (2nd Saturday)
Contact: Texas Open, 2050 N. Shady Oaks Dr., Southlake, TX 76092 (972) 219-3550
Lewisville Parks & Recreation

September
San Marcos, TX — Republic of Texas Chilympiad - Texas Men's State
Championship (3rd Saturday) Contact: Republic of Texas Chilympiad, PO Box 188,
San Marcos, TX 78667 (512) 396-5400 or http://www.aniom.net/chilympiad

October
Irving, TX — Chili Society, Ltd. Chili/BBQ Cook-off (1st Saturday)
Contact: Leukemia Society, 12850 Spurling Rd. #190, Dallas, TX 75230-1258
(972) 239-0959 or fax 239-0892

Las Vegas, NV — International Chili Society Championship Cook-off (1st Saturday)
Contact: International Chili Society, 6755 Speedway Blvd., Las Vegas, NV 89115
(877) 777-4ICS - (777-4427) or fax (702) 643-5777 http://www.chilicookoff.com

Luckenbach, TX — Ladies State Chili Championship of Texas (1st Saturday)
Contact: Susie Higgins, 613 Willow Creek, San Marcos, TX 78666 (512) 396-4456

Ruidoso, NM — New Mexico State Open Chili Cook-off (1st Saturday)
Contact: Ruidoso Chili Society, PO Box 280, Ruidoso, NM 88345
(505) 257-5123 Paul Crown

Yorktown, TX — Charlie's Western Days Chili Cook-off (3rd Saturday)
Contact: Yorktown Chamber of Commerce, PO Box 488, Yorktown, TX 78164
(512) 564-2661

Flatonia, TX — Czhilispiel (4th Saturday)
Contact: Chamber of Commerce, PO Box 651, Flatonia, TX 78941 (512) 865-3920

November
Terlingua, TX — CASI Terlingua International Chili Cook-off (1st Saturday)
Contact: Johnye Harriman, 10906 E CR 108, Midland, TX 79706-5366 (915) 620-0725 (eve) or http://www.chili.org

Terlingua, TX — Original Terlingua International, Frank X. Tolbert - Wick Fowler Memorial Championship Chili Cook-off (1st Saturday)
Contact: Viva Terlingua Headquarters, PO Box 617, Corsicana, TX 75151-0617 (903) 874-5601 phone and fax

Clarion of the Chili & BBQ World
Debbie Eiland Turner, Editor / Publisher

The *Goat Gap Gazette* is a newspaper mainly for chili and BBQ cooks, and their ilk. It comes out 12 months a year. Nothing serious is included in its columns. We hope.

The paper was started in 1974 by John Raven to keep chiliheads informed of happenings. It has grown to include Chili and BBQ cook-off listings, winners, photos, gossip, and articles. Readers are invited to submit information and photos for publication.

Cook-offs are listed 3 months for free.

Advertise your cook-off or product in the newspaper. Call or write for prices and sizes of ads, discounts for multi-month ads.

Goat Gap Gazette * PO Box 800 * Brookesmith, TX 76827-0800
915 / 646-6914 or FAX 915 / 646-8564

Chapter IV

Canned Chili

Learn to make great chili.

H. Jackson Brown Jr.

$\mathcal{M}$ost foods lend themselves to canning, and given the state of today's technology, virtually every kind of food is. We have canned meats, vegetables, fruits, and drinks. "If it can be eaten, it can be canned," said a representative of one of the country's leading canning companies during a recent speech.

Entire meals can also be canned, and the inventory of soups, stews, and other things encountered at supermarkets these days appears endless. It was inevitable, therefore, that chili would be found in a can. In fact, the history of canned chili represents an amazing success story. Furthermore, a frightening truth is that most of the chili consumed in the United States—indeed, in the world—comes out of a can.

Food consumer groups began keeping statistics on canned chili in 1948. During that year, according to the data, 81.3 million pounds of canned chili was produced. By the mid-1970s, this figure had risen to 220 million pounds, and the most recent unofficial data available at this writing suggests that the annual production now exceeds 260 million pounds per year. These statistics do not include the smaller mom and pop chili canneries, many of which operate around the country and only distribute intrastate. Likewise, the figures omit the many millions of pounds of chili that are manufactured in bulk for

the nation's Armed Forces. Furthermore, these statistics do not include brick chili.

So, who is eating all this canned chili?

As it turns out, more canned chili is sold in New York City than in the entire state of Texas, a fact which comes as no surprise to Texans and other serious eaters of chili. In the first place, committed chilistos would never consider eating canned chili if a pot of the homemade variety was available. In the second place, it can be argued, and successfully, we think, that the majority of New York City residents probably do not know what constitutes an authentic bowl of chili.

One of the oldest canned chili companies in America is Wolf Brand Chili, a Texas-based outfit that has been in business for over a hundred years. Wolf Brand was founded by rancher and meat market owner Lyman T. Davis. As a sixteen-year-old in 1895, Davis was so impressed by the chili made by his father's ranch cook that he reproduced the recipe, filled large kettles with it, and hauled it by wagon into the town of Corsicana to sell to growing numbers of customers. Davis' chili consisted of high-grade, lean beef, several different kinds of chile peppers, spices, and a little bit of oat flour for thickening. Davis' chili sold for a nickel a bowl, and the price included crackers. Not long afterward, young Davis purchased a butcher shop and soon began producing and selling the chili on the premises.

Lyman Davis' chili business grew and grew. Not only was he supplying chili for his regular customers, he was also supplying some of it to area cafes. In time, Davis' patrons began asking for chili in a container to take home so they could eat it later. In those days, no one possessed a refrigerator, so Davis began designing ways for his customers to keep the chili for an extended period of time. Initially, in response to this need, he produced dried bricks of chili—all

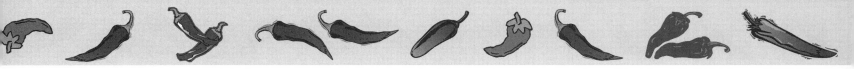

you had to do was place the brick in a pot, add water, and heat it up.

Around this time, Davis also experimented with canning. He purchased an inexpensive canning machine, but it kept breaking down. A short time later Davis hired a local man named Fred Slauson to repair and maintain the machine and as a result began producing quantities of canned chili. Slauson eventually became a full-time, permanent employee.

In 1908, according to the late Francis X. Tolbert, William Gebhardt produced the first commercial canned chili. This is only partly true. Though Lyman Davis had been selling canned chili before Gebhardt, the latter was actually the first to introduce contemporary marketing techniques relative to selling this product.

Seeing the success of Davis and Gebhardt, other companies entered the canned chili production business. A few of them followed traditional chili recipes, but several cut corners and used inferior cuts of meat including eyeballs, gums, lips, gristle, fat, and testicles.

By 1921 Davis was selling and shipping his product around the state of Texas. In 1922 he named his chili Lyman's Famous Wolf Brand Chili in honor of his pet wolf, Kaiser Bill. Davis initially planned to name his product Kaiser Bill Chili, but in a seizure of good sense he decided against it.

For years Wolf Brand Chili was sold only in Texas. Some Arkansawyers, Oklahomans, and Louisianans alive during the 1920s and 1930s can recall acquiring bootleg Wolf Brand Chili.

Though his chili company prospered, Davis accidentally discovered oil on his ranch in the late 1920s and decided to heed the call of the nation's growing need for fossil fuels. At the first opportunity, he sold his company to canning machine repairman Slauson and a local businessman named J.T. West and devoted the rest of his life to counting his millions of dollars in oil royalties.

Slauson and West shortened the name of the product to Wolf Brand Chili and hired a number of salesmen to peddle the product throughout Southwest Texas. The salesmen were equipped with chili can-shaped Model T Fords that pulled wheeled cages, each containing a large, vicious-looking wolf. The salesmen told prospective buyers that the well-fed, healthy-looking creatures dined entirely on a diet of Wolf Brand Chili and nothing else.

When Texans went off to World War II, many of them longed for a hot, steaming bowl of Wolf Brand Chili and often wrote letters home expressing a keen desire for some of the Texas product. On learning of this, Slauson and West began sending free chili to the soldiers. Even today, Wolf Brand Chili, as well as other canned chili companies, ship hundreds of cases overseas to military posts as well as to oil fields in the Middle East.

The noted Oklahoma humorist Will Rogers actively promoted Wolf Brand Chili. Once on a nationally broadcast radio show, Rogers bemoaned the fact that he was rarely able to find a decent bowl of chili during his travels around America. At the first opportunity, he said, he would journey to Corsicana and purchase several cases of Wolf Brand Chili.

In 1947 Slauson and West sold Wolf Brand Chili to Nabisco, and today it is owned by Hunt-Wesson, who claims the product is still made like it was over one hundred years ago.

Regardless of the claims, the canned chili found on the shelves of supermarkets today hardly resembles the canned chili of only two or three decades ago. Lean meat is rare, and fillers are common. Importantly, and to paraphrase Joe Cooper, canned chili is not genuine, authentic chili. Serious chili eaters eschew the product and criticize the lack of meat, the addition of chicken parts, the poor quality of beef cuts, absence of certain seasonings, and the excessive use of thickenings and water.

Much to the dismay of serious chilistos, federal regulations regarding canned chili allow the use of cheek meat, head meat, and heart meat. Lean cuts of chuck or sirloin are rare to nonexistent in canned chilis.

Today, Wolf Brand Chili is made in Tennessee. The ingredients, according to a label on a can of Wolf Brand Chili, no beans, are "meat, water, tomato puree, rolled oats, chile pepper, textured soy flour, salt, sugar, spices, garlic powder, caramel color, sodium tripolyphosphate." It is noteworthy that the fourth and sixth ingredients are thickeners, or fillers. A recent taste test involving several major brands of canned chili concluded most of them tasted "salty" and contained what appeared to be a lot of fat. In truth, none of today's canned chilis sold in supermarkets received a high rating.

With the incredible success of Wolf Brand Chili, it was inevitable it would be copied. It wasn't long before other canned chilis hit the market, chilis produced by independent manufacturers as well as major food corporations. A recent perusal of the canned chili section of a local supermarket revealed several brands including Armour, Austex, Bryan, Chilli Man, Hormel, Kelly's, and Ranch Style.

Though all of these brands taste like most people expect canned chili to taste, there were some significant differences among the leading brands in ingredients, as well as in amounts of fat, calories, cholesterol, carbohydrates, and protein.

Armour's Chili, no beans, listed water as the first ingredient, followed by "beef, mechanically separated chicken, wheat flour, spices, food starch, less than 2 percent natural flavorings, sugar, paprika, caramel coloring, salt, monosodium glutamate, textured soy protein." Once again filler—in this case, wheat flour—was a principal ingredient. During a taste test, the samplers commented the taste of the wheat flour was apparent.

Austex Chili, no beans, contained "beef and beef heart meat, water, tomatoes, rolled oats, textured vegetable protein, chile pepper, salt, sugar, and spices."

Most ingredients and portions of same were similar among all the canners with some few exceptions. For example, the first three ingredients in Hormel Chili, no beans, were water, beef, and "cereal." Cereal was also the third ingredient in Ranch Style Chili, no beans.

Those who are concerned about fat and cholesterol may be troubled by canned chili. On the other hand, some say that if one is concerned in the least bit about such things, they shouldn't be eating chili at all, at least not the traditional kind cooked with beef suet.

Recently, several of the leading brands of canned chili were studied and ranked according to fat content, total calories, calories from fat, cholesterol, carbohydrates, and protein. The name brands included in the study were Armour, Austex, Bryan, Chilli Man, Hormel, Kelly's, Ranch Style, and Wolf Brand. Results were based on a serving size of one cup.

Regarding total fat (measured in grams), the samples ranged from forty-one down to only nine:

	total fat (grams)
Austex	41
Kelly's	30
Wolf Brand	30
Chilli Man	27
Bryan	25
Armour	21
Ranch Style	14
Hormel	9

Austex, with the highest amount of fat, lists "beef heart meat" as one of its principal ingredients. Hormel, the lowest ranked in the category of total fat lists water as its first ingredient.

Austex is also the leader in total calories, Hormel again ranking last in this category:

	total calories
Austex	530
Wolf Brand	420
Kelly's	410
Chilli Man	380
Bryan	360
Armour	320
Ranch Style	280
Hormel	210

The category calories from fat also shows Austex the leader and Hormel with the least amount. The rankings are:

	calories from fat
Austex	370
Kelly's	270
Wolf Brand	270
Chilli Man	250
Bryan	230
Armour	190
Ranch Style	120
Hormel	80

The rankings for cholesterol, expressed in milligrams, are as follows:

	cholestrol (milligrams)
Wolf Brand	80
Armour	75

Chilli Man	60
Ranch Style	60
Austex	50
Kelly's	50
Bryan	50
Hormel	35

Total carbohydrates, expressed in grams, are as follows:

	carbohydrates (grams)
Kelly's	22
Austex	21
Ranch Style	21
Wolf Brand	20
Armour	17
Hormel	17
Chilli Man	16
Bryan	15

Protein, expressed in grams, is ranked as follows:

	protein (grams)
Wolf Brand	22
Chilli Man	21
Bryan	20
Austex	19
Ranch Style	19
Armour	16
Hormel	16
Kelly's	14

Regardless of how one perceives canned chili, it has become a ubiquitous element on supermarket shelves and enjoys impressive sales and consumption rates. Though not regarded as authentic by the purists, tens of thousands of pots of canned chili simmer on stoves around the country during the winter months. Each year, tens of thousands of hot dogs are covered with canned chili. Tank carloads of the stuff are served in public school lunchrooms, mixed with macaroni, and topped with Fritos. Untold quantities are spooned into bowls at hunting camps.

Like it or not, and the majority of Americans like it, canned chili has become a cultural institution in the United States.

Chapter V
The Fixin's

Cool autumn evenings cause my thoughts to turn to killin' a hog, cuttin' firewood, and cookin' up a big pot o' chili.

Anonymous

When one enters and explores the ranks of America's chili cooks, one discovers a myriad of confusion relative to fixin's. "Fixin's" is essentially a Texas word and, in this case, synonymous with what some folks call "makin's" and others simply call "stuff." Fixin's, makin's, and stuff all refer, of course, to chili ingredients and accompaniments.

The quality of your chili will depend, in large part, on what you put into it. In addition to the attitude and emotion you invest in a good pot of chili, the actual fixin's you include can make you or break you. The right fixin's, prepared with care, can elevate you from an average chili cook to one with distinction and honor. Poor or inadequate fixin's can ruin not only a pot of chili quicker than a rain shower can ruin a picnic, it can also ruin reputations and make pariahs out of otherwise good folks.

Fixin's includes meat, peppers, other vegetables, spices, and even liquids. To some people, God bless and protect them, fixin's can even mean beans.

Meat

Let's get one thing straight up front: Chili is a meat dish, period. The term *chili con carne* means, literally, chili with meat. It should be clear to all that the meat represents the major ingredient in traditional chili, both in terms of quantity and, to a large degree, in determining taste.

Virtually any kind of meat can be used in preparing chili, but beef is the most common. Joe Cooper always insisted it must be mature beef, but practiced chili cooks are able to concoct an excellent pot of chili with cheaper cuts of meat. Many have experimented and, in fact, arrived at some fine pots of chili using meat from armadillo, rattlesnake, venison, pork, goat, lamb, antelope, buffalo, turkey, chicken, jackrabbit, and even opossum and horse meat. I even heard about some pretty good chili made with kangaroo meat! During the 1960s while working on a ranch in West Texas, I recall eating chili made from bull testicles, and quite frankly, it was darned tasty. Veal, on the other hand, generally makes a poor chili.

Regardless of your particular meat preferences, the first choice of any serious chilihead is beef. While virtually any and all kinds, cuts, and grades of beef have been used for making chili, lean is preferred. Sirloin and sirloin tip are found as often as any other cut, perhaps more, and dozens of prize winning chili recipes include it. A nice arm, blade, or shoulder chuck roast can also yield some spectacular results.

Quite acceptable chili can be made from less expensive cuts like round steak, and if one is on a budget, such cuts can prove quite satisfactory. By all means avoid cheap fatty cuts and gristle.

A lot of people around the country have been led to believe that good chili is actually made from hamburger. Depending on whom you are feeding, you might be able to get by on hamburger, but among serious chili cooks only

Philistines would do such a thing. Joe Cooper once wrote, "Only barbarians and Yankees make [chili] with ground meat."

According to culinary statistics gathered over the years, most of those who use hamburger are found in the American South. A slightly lesser number have been identified and located in the Midwest, the Great Lakes States, and the Northeast. Given what some of these folks do to chili, using hamburger as chili meat is among the least of their sins.

Let's examine this business of cubed chili meat and how it should be readied for the skillet or pot. Chili experts are in general agreement that the lean meat should be *cubed*, not finely ground. If there were such a thing as chili police, those who use hamburger would be subject to severe penalties and large fines.

The cubes should be no more than one-half-inch by one-half-inch, perhaps even slightly smaller. Several chili cooks we know prefer quarter-inch cubes. You can easily cube the meat yourself with a sharp knife or you can have your butcher do it for you. Usually, there is no extra charge for such things at good meat markets. In addition to beef, other meats employed in the preparation of chili are best cubed. Some parts of the chicken and most of the rattlesnake, however, do not lend themselves well to being cut into one-half-inch cubes. Just do the best you can.

If you do not care for cubed meat, try coarse-grinding it. Many butcher shops and supermarkets throughout Texas and the Southwest commonly offer what is called "chili grind," preground lean meat ideal for making chili. Do not confuse chili grind with hamburger. In chili grind, the individual pieces of meat are larger than hamburger and somewhat smaller than the aforementioned cubes but, all in all, wind up being quite satisfactory. Our experience suggests that chili grind is virtually unknown and largely unavailable outside of this geographic region.

Chile Peppers

While beef is the heart of chili, chile peppers are the soul.

When peppers are used in the making of chili, the cook is faced with an embarrassment of riches, for there is a wide variety from which to choose. Many cooks have their favorites and employ them over and over. Others vary the kinds of chile peppers used in their chili to provide different tastes. Experimenting with different chiles is fun, can't hurt you, and does not break any laws. The process of discovery is important here and ultimately can lead to some fine results.

Technically, chiles are not peppers in the strictest sense of the word. Bell peppers are true peppers. The confusion arose when Christopher encountered chiles in the Caribbean Islands: He misidentified them as peppers and the term "chile peppers" has been with us ever since. The early Spanish conquistadors added somewhat to the confusion. When they arrived among the Incas and ate some of the food prepared for them, they believed the strong spice in the various dishes came from a kind of black pepper they knew from back home. Thereafter, the Spaniards, like Columbus, called the chiles peppers.

Though different varieties are now grown across the world, chiles are uniquely American in origin. Happily, several regional cuisines have benefitted from the more than two hundred varieties of chile peppers known to exist.

The so-called heat associated with chiles comes from the veins and membranes in the pod and not from the seeds as so many people believe. As a general rule, the more pointed the chile, the hotter it is. Likewise, on the average, the smaller the chile, the hotter it tends to be. When preparing peppers, fresh or dried, for chili, stems, seeds, and peels are normally removed and discarded.

Chile peppers, first and foremost, provide flavor for chili con carne. The heat is merely a by-product, although many believe chili is not authentic unless it is

hot. Heat, to be sure, can add a dimension to chili but never at the expense of, or substitute for, flavor.

The active ingredient in chile peppers that provides the heat is an alkaloid named *capsaicin*, and the genus to which chiles are assigned is *Capsicum*.

The peppers used in making chili can be found in supermarkets and specialty stores fresh, dried, ground, powdered, canned, or, rarely, in paste form. They can be selected from the many varieties of chile peppers or, for the less adventurous and/or those with tender stomachs, from different kinds of bell peppers. Chili powder, made from chile and other ingredients, is such an important element that it will be treated independently later on in this chapter.

When using fresh peppers, it is best to chop or dice and sauté them early during the preparation of the chili, or puree them, depending on the recipe. They can easily be sautéed along with the onions and garlic.

For those who like a hotter or more robust chili, additional diced and raw fresh chiles are sometimes added later during the simmering. They can simply be tossed into the pot and stirred into the concoction or added as a topping on serving. The amount depends on you. Or your fellow diners.

Here's another suggestion: Before using fresh chiles, make certain they are peeled. If not, the peels will work loose during the cooking process. They are not particularly tasty or desirable. We have also been told that chile pepper peels are not digested.

Some folks also like to roast their chiles before adding them to the pot, and roasting not only adds flavor but can be helpful in peeling the chile. Roasting can be done over a barbecue grill or in an oven turned up to around 400 degrees. When the skin on the peppers begin to blister, pull them out and peel the skins away.

When handling chiles, particularly extremely hot ones like habaneros and jalapeños, refrain from rubbing your eyes or genital area. You could be very

sorry you did. Some who handle chile peppers a lot suggest that buttering your hands and fingers keeps them safe from the burning effect of the *capsaicin*. We have tried this and found it to be minimally effective. It is recommended here that you wear rubber gloves while working with hot chiles. When finished, wash both the gloves and your hands and fingers in hot, soapy water. If you do experience severe burns from the *capsaicin*, treat the affected area with a paste made from baking soda and water, a commercial salve, or even a fresh piece of aloe vera.

To counteract the heat left by the chiles in your mouth, try dairy products such as milk or cheese along with the chili.

Here are a few chile peppers worth considering in the making of chili.

Anaheim

The Anaheim, also called the California chile, is a green chile and grows to a length of approximately seven inches. The Anaheim has a pleasant, mild taste and, while a favorite for many, is sometimes considered a bit tame for those who like their chili really hot. When used in chili, the Anaheim is often accompanied by other, hotter chiles. When dried, the Anaheim takes on a deep reddish color. These days, one can usually find fresh Anaheims in the produce section of any good supermarket. They can also be found canned and are generally labeled "green chiles."

Ancho

Ancho is a Spanish term for "wide," and indeed these tasty peppers are wide near the stem, tapering toward the end and forming a kind of triangle. Anchos are the dried version of poblanos, and they are wide pods about four inches long. They range from dark red to almost black in color. As chiles go, anchos are not unacceptably hot for most folks. The ancho is generally the favored

pepper for chili, being just a bit hotter than the popular Anaheim and, according to many, considerably tastier. In California and along the west coast of Mexico, the ancho is called a pasilla. This is sometimes confusing, since a true pasilla is a relatively narrow, six-inch long brownish chile pepper.

The poblano, if not dried and used in chili as ancho, is a favorite ingredient in a number of delicious pork stews.

Arbol

Powdered chile arbol can sometimes be found in specialty stores and is a desired ingredient for chili among a number of devoted chiliheads. The arbol, a close relative of the cayenne, grows to about three inches in length and when mature is a fiery red-orange color. This somewhat hot chile also offers a delicious taste and provides a bit of fire to your pot of chili. It is not for sissies.

Cayenne

Cayenne peppers are infrequently used in chili except in the powdered form. This thin, red pepper, between four to seven inches long, tends to be hot yet quite flavorful. The cayenne has become extremely popular in parts of Asia and is used extensively in a variety of different cuisines.

Guajillo

The guajillo pepper is occasionally found in Mexican specialty food stores and is generally labeled "mirasol." It is an orange-red to brown pepper, tapered, about five inches long, and one-and-a-half inches wide. The guajillo has a sweeter taste than most chiles.

Habanero

According to scientists who study such things, the habanero, looking deceptively like a miniature, shriveled bell pepper, is the hottest chile in the world.

Long used in cooking in Mexico, the habanero has grown in popularity in the United States in recent years such that it is now sometimes found in the fresh produce sections of good supermarkets. Small amounts of habanero pepper are often used in Texas-style barbecue sauces. If you are compelled to add habanero peppers to your chili, remember that a little bit goes a long way. Only a few hardy and tough-throated cooks regularly use them in chili these days.

Jalapeño

Due to the growing popularity of Tex-Mex cuisine around the country, even the world, the jalapeño has become a rather ubiquitous chile. One reason for its popularity is simply related to the fact that it is darned tasty, though much too hot for those with very tender palates. Always common in Texas and the Southwest, jalapeños can be found these days in supermarkets as far north as Montana. A friend who lives in Connecticut happily reported that jalapeños are now available in Hartford.

Jalapeños grow to three inches long and are picked while they are green. Left to ripen on the plant, they will turn red. They can be purchased fresh, canned, and frozen. Fresh is always best, but if not available, the other versions are not bad. For those who like their chili hot and also like the taste of jalapeños, fresh ones are generally chopped or minced and added to the pot during the last half hour of cooking. Dried and crushed jalapeños are not as ubiquitous in stores as are fresh and canned ones but can be found in some specialty shops.

Also growing in popularity are chipotles, which are dried and smoked jalapeños. Chipotles added to chili provide not only the heat desired by many, but also a rich smoky flavor unlike anything else.

New Mexico

The New Mexico chile has been described as a hybrid and is fast becoming very popular with chili cooks around the country. Similar and closely related to an Anaheim, the New Mexico chile offers rich, robust flavor with a significant amount of heat. New Mexico chiles come in green and red and can be found fresh, dried, frozen, and powdered.

Pasilla

A more common name for the pasilla is *chile negro* because of its dark, almost black, color. Looking much like an Anaheim, the pasilla is fairly spicy and hot, smells a bit like raisins, and is considered by a number of chiliheads as a serious chile pepper. Pasilla is often used as an ingredient in chili powders.

Pequins

Chile pequins are tiny, almost raisin-sized and -shaped chiles, often found growing wild along portions of the Texas-Mexico border. Some chili historians believe that the pequin was the first chile used in making chili for the cowhands during early trail drive days in Texas. They are still favored by those who like their chili good and hot. In fact, a number of purists claim that any chili made without pequins is not authentic.

Poblano

See ancho.

Scotch Bonnet

This little chile pepper looks a lot like a habanero and is just about as hot. Although occasionally used in chili recipes, the scotch bonnet is not particularly common in the United States and offers no substantial improvement over the more common habanero.

Serrano

Serrano chiles have also been growing in popularity lately among those who like a hot pepper. This rather thin, two-inch-long chile is a bit hotter than a jalapeño and has found many fans among those who like a hot chili. Serranos, like a few other kinds of chiles, can be found pickled and for sale in a variety of supermarkets. They can be quite hot but are also quite flavorful.

Onions

Regardless of how you may feel about onions, many believe you cannot make real chili without them. Some, however, eschew them altogether. Ultimately, personal tastes and preferences should be your guide here. As with chiles, a wide variety of onions is available.

After years of observation, it appears that yellow onions are the most commonly used in chili. This seems quite appropriate, for yellow onions are quite tasty and inexpensive.

Some folks prefer purple or red onions. Purples and reds offer a somewhat different flavor than yellows and work rather well in chili. Purples and reds tend to be slightly more expensive than yellows but not prohibitively so.

Some chiliheads prefer sweet-tasting onions like Vidalias. Available in most fine grocery stores, Vidalias have a great flavor and can do some wonderful things to a pot of chili.

I have eaten chili prepared with green onions, leeks, and scallions. While I didn't find this too objectionable, I found that these varieties simply lack the contribution, the robustness, and the punch of a good yellow onion.

The size to which the onions are cut up varies, and heated arguments have been waged over this subject. Some like to dice the onion real fine before sautéing it. This, they claim, enables the tiny pieces to practically dissolve in the pot. Others, and I am among them, prefer the onion chopped into pieces

approximately the size of your smallest fingernail before sautéing. Some of us care little about having our onions virtually disappear into the liquid, preferring instead to experience the direct taste and texture of this wonderful and oh-so-versatile vegetable.

It must be pointed out here that the presence of visible pieces and chunks of vegetables, such as onion, in a pot or bowl of chili is not tolerated in most cook-offs. As a result, many chili cooks resort to powdered or minced onion as a substitute for fresh ones.

Tomatoes

Discussion of tomatoes as an ingredient to authentic chili can be a dangerous undertaking. Purists and traditionalists do not use tomatoes in the making of chili and push away any bowl o' red that contains this particular fruit. (Yes, it is true; the tomato is a fruit, not a vegetable.) World renowned chilisto Joe Cooper once quoted E. DeGolyer as stating that the use of tomatoes in chili, ripe or canned, was regarded as "effeminate." Cooper further claimed that the presence of tomato actually detracts from the flavor provided by the chile pepper.

Whether or not you believe in the use of tomatoes in chili, the fact remains, however unpleasant it may be for some of you, that a number of world champion recipes employ them as an ingredient or as a topping or garnish. A number of such recipes are included in this book.

Some claim to use tomato for taste, some argue it is for color, and others maintain they add it for texture. A few who do not employ tomato in the actual cooking of the chili will sometimes apply chopped tomato as a garnish.

For those of you who do use tomatoes, fresh is best. This should go without saying. There are, in fact, few things better than a homegrown tomato. Unfortunately, many who do not have their own gardens are forced to purchase tomatoes at supermarkets. Supermarket tomatoes, on the whole, tend to be an

unsatisfactory product. Most tomatoes one finds in grocery stores these days are hydroponically grown—that is, they are essentially laboratory tomatoes grown in a slurry that circulates beneath a rack which holds the fruit. The roots of these poor little tomato plants never touch soil. As a result, supermarket tomatoes have the taste and personality of a piece of cardboard. You would be just as well served to purchase canned tomatoes.

If tomatoes are used, and you can't get homegrowns, virtually any kind will do as long as they are juicy. Make certain you peel them—tomato peels in chili are as unwanted and unloved as chile pepper peels. An advantage to using canned tomatoes is that they are already peeled. Many have found happiness in using canned tomatoes, which are at least as good as and generally better than supermarket produce section tomatoes.

Tomato in some form is often employed as a liquid. Some will use tomato sauce, while others favor tomato juice. Spicy tomato juice cocktail has even been employed from time to time.

A caution is required here: If you are a tomato user, be careful not to overdo it. Too much tomato can ruin the flavor of a pot of chili.

Another word of caution: We have learned that some misguided souls substitute catsup for tomato in their chili recipes. This is not something that should be admitted in polite society. Catsup offers few, if any, positives for a bowl of chili but does add a host of negatives, mostly relating to ingredients such as sugar and preservatives.

Other Vegetables

More and more these days we are encountering chili recipes that contain additional vegetables such as celery, carrots, corn, and bell peppers. Depending on what the other ingredients are, these relative newcomers to chili can, in fact, impart a totally acceptable and a somewhat complimentary taste, but chances are your chili will not suffer from the absence of them. If there existed an important vegetable ingredient for chili other than chile peppers, onions, and the other usual stuff, we would have learned about it by now.

Chili traditionalists insist there is no place whatsoever for the likes of celery, carrots, corn, and bell peppers and recommend you refrain from experimenting with same. Several recipes that call for these ingredients, however, are not half bad, and a few have been included in this book.

Herbs and Spices

Spices, as they relate to chili, are often misunderstood. It is true that a wide variety of spices and seasonings are tossed into chili pots around the country, but many of them are not necessary. The secret is not in the number of spices used, but in the *blend*. Traditionally, the most successful blend of spices, as it relates to chili powder, consists of salt, pepper (red or black), chili powder (see below), cumin, garlic, occasionally oregano, and sometimes paprika. There will be those who would argue with this list, but it happens to be the result of years of research.

Other seasonings, however, have been employed with good results. Below we present an inventory. In case you need to refer to this section in the future, they are listed in alphabetical order so your search will be made easier.

Basil

Basil, sometimes sweet basil, is occasionally used in chili. If tomatoes are employed in the preparation of the chili, basil is recommended since it compliments the tomato. Otherwise, you will hurt nothing to just leave it out.

Bay leaf

A bay leaf or two can be added to your chili if you like. While a bay leaf floating on top of a pot of chili might look good to some, I personally have never been convinced it contributes a single thing to the taste. If you do use a bay leaf, remember to remove it before serving.

Cayenne

Cayenne pepper in the powdered form is becoming a common ingredient in chili. Since cayenne supplies more heat than taste, use it instead of, not in addition to, other peppers such as jalapeño or habanero.

Cilantro

Cilantro, also called Chinese parsley, Mexican parsley, and coriander (coriander is the seed of the plant that yields cilantro), is in great demand these days as a result of the growing popularity of Tex-Mex food. Since cilantro adds to the flavor of a wide variety of such cuisine, many believe it will also be suitable for use in chili. I rather like cilantro and have found a small amount works well in chili, but it depends on how it is used. When serving, try sprinkling a bit of cilantro atop the chili—the taste can be most appreciated in this manner. Cooking cilantro with the chili is a waste of time and good seasoning.

Cumin

Next to black pepper, cumin is the most popular seasoning in the world. No serious chili cook would dare prepare a bowl of red without cumin. Cumin comes powdered and as whole seeds. Here is something I learned a long time ago. If you can get seeds, try roasting them in the oven (or searing them in a skillet) for several minutes. Following this, grind them up and add the requisite amount to your chili. The fresher the seeds the better, and they are hard to beat for taste.

Garlic

Without wishing to generate an argument, let me state that garlic, though technically a vegetable, is also an herb. The addition of garlic to chili is done from an herbal and seasoning point of view, hence its inclusion in this section. There are several varieties of garlic, ranging from sweet to pungent, and the only rule here is to use the amount you like best.

Professional chili cooks use garlic cloves minced well before sautéing. Some cooks have successfully employed granulated and powdered garlic to good effect. These alternatives work well and are easy to use but somehow lack the full-bodied flavor of the fresh cloves. My opinion is that the mincing of a couple of fresh garlic cloves is well worth the effort if you are interested in cooking a serious pot of chili.

Oregano

Oregano is considered by many to be an essential ingredient for chili. I particularly like the taste of this seasoning, purchase Mexican oregano in bulk, and use it liberally in chili as well as in a variety of sauces and stews. To my way of thinking, however, you have to use a lot of oregano in chili if you want to taste it. While I regularly use oregano in my recipes, some argue that chili would not suffer much if it were left out.

Paprika

Ground paprika is a welcome and desirable ingredient in a lot of chili recipes. Paprika is actually a pepper, and while some of us like it for the taste, others use it for color. I prefer Hungarian paprika over Mexican simply because it is stronger. If available, try smoked paprika in your next batch of chili—it offers a robust taste that has delighted legions of chili eaters.

Salt

Salt is a necessary ingredient for chili. Salt can bring out the true flavor of meat like no other seasoning. If you are on a salt-free diet, you don't need to be eating chili unless you can find a suitable substitute. Most of us use plain old table salt, but for a slightly exotic and altogether pleasant taste, try sea salt. Sea salt is generally found in health food stores and a few good supermarkets.

Thyme

Thyme is rarely added to chili, but in the few recipes that call for it, this herb, used sparingly, imparts an interesting and quite acceptable flavor.

Woodruff

Woodruff is a seasoning found in the recipes of Woody DeSilva and Ormly Gumfudgin, but it is not readily available on grocery store shelves. Gumfudgin informs me that woodruff is the first seasoning mentioned in the Bible. Regardless, only a few chili cooks have ever heard of it, even fewer ever use it, and some argue it has no place in chili at all.

Most of us who are concerned about quality when it comes to the preparations of foods, particularly chili, purchase our seasonings from supply houses instead of grocery stores. The difference in taste and quality is clear.

Furthermore, purchasing seasonings in bulk from a well-established supply house will save you lots of money. Two good ones are Pendry's in Fort Worth, Texas, 304 E. Belknap, 972/442-2555 or 800/533-1870 and Penzeys in Wisconsin, PO Box 933, Muskego, WI 53150, 414/679-7207.

Chili Powder

Beginning chili cooks often confuse chili powder with powdered chiles. Not all chili powders are the same. Commercial chili powders vary somewhat according to manufacturer, but as a rule, they contain powdered chile pepper, cumin, oregano, and garlic powder, although the portions of each is not consistent among suppliers. Some add salt, some don't.

Traditionally, powdered ancho chiles are most often found in commercial chili powders, but growing interest in chili cooking has led to the use of other types of peppers, such as pasilla. Some adventurous souls even add a half-teaspoon or so of habanero powder to the mix just for some added zing.

If you are compelled to use the commercial chili powders you find on the supermarket shelves rather than make your own, it is recommended you stick with well-known brands. It pays to go with quality. Several lesser-known brands of chili powder tend to be inferior and ultimately lead to an inferior pot of chili.

Some advanced levels of chili cooking often call for powdered chile, not chili powder. Pure chile powders come in a number of varieties, including New Mexico, ancho, Anaheim, California, and pasilla. A few new hybrids are also growing in popularity. The purest of the purists purchase the whole dried chile pods and grind or puree their own.

The type of chili powder and powdered chile you use is best arrived at via experimentation, one of my favorite parts of cooking chili.

Sweeteners

When one examines chili recipes that come out of the South, one discovers that sugar is a common ingredient. Since most truly serious chili cooks I know would rather be stabbed than put sugar in a pot of red, this baffled me for years until I discovered the reason. For one, Southerners put sugar in everything—chili, greens, soups, stews, and other dishes. It appears to be a cultural habit for many of them, one that is apparently not easily broken. While many would regard adding sugar to chili as a sacrilege, I have heard one or two compelling arguments in favor of it.

If you are violently opposed to sweeteners, just calm down and bear with me for a moment. A lot of people, among them some mighty impressive and championship chili cooks, add a bit of sugar or some other sweetener to chili. This is done, as one stated, "to round out and subdue what can be harsh or biting flavors of the chili powder, paprika, and chile peppers." In fact, some world championship chili recipes actually call for a small amount of sugar.

For my part, I love, even crave, the unsugared flavor of chili powder, paprika, and chile peppers, but I also appreciate the notion that some are more sensitive to them than I.

I tried experimenting with sugar and other sweeteners with a few pots of chili over the years but ultimately rejected them. If, however, you must have some kind of sweetener, let me offer a couple of suggestions. Stay away from ordinary table sugar and try brown sugar. I even tried using honey once and found it to work OK. A friend once recommended a tablespoonful of cocoa powder. I tried it, it was better than plain sugar, but I'll never do it again.

Those who come from the round-out-and-subdue-the-biting-flavors school of thought but who dislike sugar in chili as much as I do have discovered other effective ingredients, including chocolate, cinnamon, coffee, and molasses.

Liquids

Since chili is essentially a kind of stew, some amount of liquid is required. Some folks simply use water, which works just fine. Some rely on the juice from tomatoes, fresh or canned. Those who need to add liquids, but are deeply concerned with taste, have discovered a number of alternatives.

We are seeing beef broth and chicken broth cropping up more and more often in some good chili recipes. I've used chicken broth from time to time, splashing a bit into the cooking pot when fluids get low, and rather like it. The broth adds a nice flavor to the chili, but you want to be careful not to overdo it.

Several championship chili recipes include beer, which, some believe, adds a nice punch. You needn't be concerned with alcohol content because most of it quickly cooks away. Should you choose to try beer the next time you need to add liquid, and I recommend you do, go for a nice dark Mexican beer such as Dos Equis or Tecate. They are so much more flavorful than American beers.

I have had chili where red wine was used for liquid. It was not bad but seemed to lend itself to a kind of yuppie chili. On the other hand, I sometimes raise the level of liquid in my chili by adding a bit of tequila and claim some delightfully tasty results. Here again, you must take care to use a high-quality tequila, not one of those brands favored by college fraternities. Examine the label on the bottle and look for information relating that what you hold in your hand is "100 percent blue agave" tequila. It makes an amazing difference.

In recent years, I have had some chili that included whiskey as a principal liquid. A half-cup of good whiskey provides a flavor like nothing else and is worth a try.

Other liquids have been used with some success. Surprisingly, a tablespoon or two of vinegar does wonders for a pot of chili, as does a similar amount of lime juice. Some use lemon juice, but the taste of lime somehow works better with chili than does lemon. Work it out among yourselves.

Cooking Oil

One of the concessions chili cooks have made in recent years is related to cooking oil. Initially, the meat was browned in fat, the favorite being kidney suet. If suet was not available, the meat was cooked in grease from bacon or salt pork, or lard. While fats provide considerably more flavor to chili than cooking oils, growing concerns relative to health and cholesterol have led to their general abandonment among many.

We have a bit of a dilemma. It is, in truth, the fat that, in large part, accounts for the taste in meat, whether barbecueing, broiling, frying, or adding to chili. A little fat is probably OK, but too much of the saturated kind consumed too often can, according to medical research, lead to health problems. As a result, even the staunchest chiliheads have weaned themselves off fat and lard and have switched to low-cholesterol cooking oils. After all, we want you around for a long time to enjoy the pleasures of a bowl of chili.

The cooking oil, of course, is generally employed in the browning of the meat. By and large, any good cooking oil will do, with extra virgin olive oil preferred by most. Canola oil is also seen more and more during chili cook-offs. I use olive oil for health considerations. I heartily recommend it, and I include it in most of my own recipes. While I have grown fond of the taste of olive oil, please feel free to substitute your own preference if it is not to your liking.

Speaking of oils and fats, a professional and highly successful chili competitor once told me for the absolute best results, use goose fat. This fat, he claims, brings out the flavor of meat like no other. Goose fat, however, does not stack up against olive and canola oils as far as health considerations are concerned and is likely not easy to obtain.

Thickenings

The use of thickenings in chili has provoked an argument or two over the past few decades. Some, who claim to be purists, simply never use thickening in their chili, claiming no decent pot of red requires a thickening agent. Others, who also claim to be purists, maintain that a bit of thickening provides an acceptable texture to the chili.

Many of us care little for thickenings, though we confess to dining on excellent pots of chili that contained such. Thickenings used in relatively large quantities can go a long way in ruining a pot of chili—look what it has done to canned chilis. I am persuaded that the employment of a thickening in your recipe is a personal matter.

If you are inclined to employ a thickening, try masa harina, a finely ground cornmeal. Masa is easily found in supermarkets throughout the Southwest and generally encountered in specialty food stores in the rest of the country. Soak a little masa overnight in some water until you achieve the consistency of a viscous paste. Squeeze a bit of lime juice into it and mix well for added effect. The next day, during the final cooking phases of your chili, add just a little bit of the masa paste at a time to the mix until you have achieved the consistency you like.

If you are unable to get masa, flour tends to be the alternative of choice. Some soak it overnight, others simply add a couple of tablespoonsful right out of the bag to the pot of chili. Other thickeners we have encountered in the past include coarse-ground cornmeal, cracker meal, and even oatmeal. Oatmeal is used most often in canned chilis, primarily as a stretcher.

Beans

A touchy subject, beans, and one that has been argued and fought about for decades. Chili purists may feel free to skip this section and go directly to the next.

Serious chili competitions absolutely forbid the use of beans. However, since many citizens of this country claim to be unable to enjoy a pot of chili without the addition of beans, we decided this may be the best place to deal with it. We will attempt to limit the discussion to quality and quantity.

There is scant evidence relative to the first use of beans in chili, but most historians suggest they were associated with a need to stretch the food during lean times, added when there was not much meat to be had. The use of beans, according to research, is most common in the South and Midwest, and less so in Texas and the Southwest.

Beans, served in a small bowl alongside one's bowl of chili, is quite traditional. In fact, it is even expected at some levels of society. If you have friends over for a chili supper, those who expect beans in their chili are completely at liberty to scoop them into their bowl while the traditionalists turn their heads.

Beans cooked *in* the chili is another matter. To many committed chili cooks, placing beans in the concoction is to invite comparison, to place oneself in the position of being completely and totally separated from the chili elite of this country. Reputations have been dashed as a result of such culinary *faux pax*, social standings have plummeted, and otherwise good people have become the butt of cruel jokes. If, however, you insist on using beans in chili, here are a few pointers.

If you must have beans, please consider the traditional and tasty pinto bean. The pinto is probably the favorite of the bean-adders, particularly west of the nation's Bean Line (see Chapter III, The Geography of Chili).

Kidney beans are often employed, and I have heard from dozens of Northerners and Easterners that kidneys taste very good in a bowl o' red, and they wouldn't have it any other way. I have had some excellent homemade chili containing kidney beans and, while not authentic, I didn't die from it. Kidney beans tend to be just a touch sweeter than pinto beans.

Red beans have also been used. In fact, some rather tasty chili I've sampled in Cajun Louisiana employed red beans. Reds, like kidneys, tend to be somewhat sweeter than the pintos.

While traveling through the South, I have encountered chili made with butter beans and even black-eyed peas! In the American Midwest, lima beans and navy beans are often added to chili.

Once in Arkansas, I was fed a bowl of chili that contained canned pork and beans!

I am convinced that, while canned beans are handy and easy, cooked dried beans work best. Soak the dried pintos (or kidneys, or reds, or limas, or whatever) overnight and cook them the next day the way you like them. Canned beans tend to be slightly mushier and contain preservatives and occasionally other ingredients you may not want in your chili recipe.

Toppings and Accompaniments

If made correctly with all of the right ingredients, a good bowl of chili doesn't need anything else. Some, however, like to "top" their chili with one or more items and serve some extras, like bread or crackers, on the side. Garnishes can add color as well as flavor, and a plate of some kind of bread nearby can also compliment the chili. Some examples of garnishes and accompaniments are offered below.

Avocado

Some like to slice avocado and lay the pieces across the top of the chili. The avocado adds a nice green color but, quite frankly, is not particularly complimentary to the other tastes found in a bowl o' red.

Catsup

Only someone who has not been exposed to authentic chili would consider adding catsup. Some canned and commercial chilis may be so bad that a dollop of catsup may actually improve them, but it is hard to imagine.

Cheese

I occasionally witness folks spreading shredded cheese across the surface of their chili. I've seen people apply cheddar, Swiss, Monterey jack, mozzarela, feta, and even parmesan. I love chili and I love cheese, but rarely do I mix the two. Quite frankly, if the chili is correctly made, cheese may actually detract from the taste. On the other hand, if the chili is bad, the cheese may help it a little.

Cilantro

Tiny amounts of cilantro are sometimes included in chili recipes, but the flavor is essentially camouflaged by other ingredients. Fresh cilantro, chopped and applied as a garnish atop a bowl of red, is quite acceptable and tasty.

Chile peppers

Fresh, chopped chiles are sometimes added as a garnish and introduced to spice up the chili. Jalapeños and serranos are commonly used for flavor and color. Pequins have been used to good effect if the effect desired was to increase the heat. Poblanos and Anaheims sliced lengthwise and laid across the top of the chili can be good.

Crackers

Crackers can be crumbled and added to chili. Some diners just drop the crumbs atop the chili as a kind of saltine garnish, whereas others mix it in. Crackers, we are told, were initially used to absorb grease, but over the years diners developed a taste for them. Crackers are also commonly eaten as a side instead of bread or corn bread.

Fritos and other chips

It was inevitable that two foods that had their origins in Texas would combine. Some folks like to add Fritos or others types of corn chips to their chili much like one would add crackers.

Olives

I have occasionally encountered a bowl of chili garnished with ripe or green olives. This has occurred mostly in the North. After several honest attempts at trying to appreciate olives in chili, I confess to concluding that there is no place for them.

Onions

Chopped green onions applied as a garnish are acceptable and offer a bit of texture and taste that appeals to some.

Parsley

Chopped fresh parsley is favored by many as a garnish and rather compliments a good bowl of chili.

Pepper sauce

At last count, there were well over one hundred different kinds of hot pepper sauces on the market. The most famous of these, I suspect, is Tabasco. Tabasco and other Tabasco-like sauces are often added as an ingredient during the chili cooking process. Other times, a few drops splashed onto the top of a serving of chili add a certain zing appreciated by many.

Sour cream

More and more I am finding restaurant chili served with a dollop of sour cream on top. Many would consider such a thing an abomination and a practice that should be halted immediately. Others actually prefer sour cream atop their chili and request it if it does not come that way. I can't imagine how this practice got started, but a number of food researchers link sour cream use in chili to the culture of the American South. Indeed, a number of Southern cookbooks that feature chili recipes almost invariably include sour cream as a topping. My attitude is—if you like sour cream, then, by all means, add it.

I have also been served chili topped with other things: croutons, bacon bits, and guacamole, for examples. If one delights in such toppings, one should have the opportunity to add them. Quite frankly, most consider they detract from the robust flavor of the chili.

Tortillas

Tortillas, both corn and flour depending on your preference, are an excellent side to accompany a bowl of chili. Some, including myself, have occasionally sliced warm corn tortillas into thin strips and garnished the top of a bowl o' red with them.

Corn bread

Corn bread is also a popular accompaniment to chili. There is something about cornmeal that accentuates the taste of chili. Sliced, buttered corn bread as a side is hard to beat. Some like to crumble their corn bread into the chili much like others do with crackers.

Oyster crackers

In some parts of the country where I have ordered chili, the bowl o' red is accompanied by oyster crackers. As with saltines and corn bread, the oyster crackers can be eaten separately or crumbled into the chili. Some claim nothing goes as well with a bowl of chili as do these little morsels.

White bread

As far as breads go, there are some folks who prefer white bread and nothing else. White bread is often a preferred accompaniment to barbecue, but we encounter a number of souls who also like it with chili. A couple of white bread enthusiasts told us there is nothing better for sopping up the delicious chili liquid from the bottom of the bowl than a slice of white bread.

Drinks

What one drinks with chili should be a matter of personal preference, and there is little agreement among chiliheads as to which is the best.

Because dairy products help ease the burn from the chile peppers, many prefer milk. Some I know can't eat a bowl of chili without a big glass of cold sweet milk nearby. I know a man who claims buttermilk is even better. Iced tea is commonly consumed with chili but lacks the soothing effect of milk. Iced water is preferred by some. Beer and hard liquor also have their adherents.

The Vessel

Occasionally, discussions arise on the best kind of vessel to use for cooking chili. There are some—H. Allen Smith for one—who maintain that you are less than civilized if you do not use a cast-iron pot. Frankly, I feel much the same way, though I have experienced good results with other types of cookware.

Somehow, cast-iron skillets and pots seem to be made for such things as fixing chili. Furthermore, I have seen an awful lot of cast-iron pots at chili cook-offs, most often among the winners. A good sign, I maintain.

However emotional you are regarding this subject, the ultimate truth is that any kind of decent, high-quality cooking vessel will work fine. Don't skimp on price—a cheap, flimsy pot will serve no good purpose at all, and can wear out in a relatively short time. A good pot—cast iron, enamel, aluminum—can last a lifetime.

Chapter VI

Recipes

*T*he chili recipes found on the following pages represent over 135 favorites, all gleaned from a collection that was begun almost four decades ago. A lot of these recipes came from family members and friends, some were mailed to me by readers during the days I penned a food column, some were developed based on available ingredients, and many were the results of delightful experimentation. Each one has been tried, tested, modified, added to, deleted from, and otherwise messed with until an optimum pot of chili, in the opinion of the cook, resulted. These recipes are herewith presented for your enjoyment and, hopefully, your culinary satisfaction.

Following the more or less conventional recipes, a number of wild game recipes are offered. Wild game—including venison, elk, buffalo, turkey, duck, and even rattlesnake and jackrabbit—often works very well in chili. Since chili is easy to make and uses inexpensive, easy to obtain, and easy to store ingredients, cooking it in camp becomes a relatively simple task. A big pot of game chili simmering over the campfire at hunting camp can be hard to beat, and some of my fondest chili memories are related to such things.

Recent concerns relative to fat and cholesterol content in our foods have encouraged many people to modify their diets for appropriate reasons. Though they depart radically from traditional recipes, varieties of vegetarian and otherwise "healthy" chilis are appearing more often on restaurant menus. Much of it

is quite tasty as well as nutritious. The vegetarian and otherwise health-related recipes included here were developed with an eye toward eliminating as much fat and cholesterol as possible without negatively impacting the taste. Since so much of the taste of a bowl of chili comes from the meat, as well as from the grease in which the meat is cooked, the challenge became a formidable one.

Lastly, we offer several "celebrity recipes," some guidelines for chili provided by friends who eminently qualify as celebrities—actors, musicians, writers, songwriters, and other types of performers.

Traditional and Nontraditional Chili

*T*he beauty of a recipe is that it is more a guideline and less an absolute set of rules. Ingredients can be added or left out according to taste. Quantities can be altered as a result of preference. Substitutions can be, and often are, made: different chile peppers can be used depending on what the diner likes best; venison or pork can be substituted for beef; some prefer ground cumin seed as opposed to powdered cumin, powdered garlic instead of minced, and so on. H. Allen Smith, the curmudgeonly chilisto of a few decades ago, put it even stronger when he stated: "Only a fool sets down precise, unalterable proportions for chili."

Auntie Clara's Bunkhouse Chili

Auntie Clara never entered a chili cook-off, but those who have dined on her chili remain convinced she would have won hands down, anytime, anywhere. Every Friday evening out on the ranch, Auntie Clara would fix a big pot of chili, let it refrigerate overnight, and on Saturday afternoon carry it, along with bowls and spoons and a big pan of fresh corn bread, to the bunkhouse so the ranch hands could enjoy a leisurely and delicious lunch. This was back in the 1950s and 1960s, and the hands said they didn't mind working on fences and windmills for ten to twelve hours a day at seventy-five dollars per month as long as they got to eat some of Auntie Clara's Bunkhouse Chili.

2	tablespoons bacon grease
3	pounds finely cubed chuck steak
1	8-ounce can tomato sauce
1	14½-ounce can beef broth
7	tablespoons chili powder
2	tablespoons onion powder
1	tablespoon crushed red pepper
2	teaspoons beef bouillon crystals
1	teaspoon chicken bouillon crystals

Salt and black pepper to taste

1½	tablespoons ground cumin
1	tablespoon garlic powder

In a large cooking pot, heat bacon grease, add meat, and cook until brown. Add tomato sauce, beef broth, three tablespoons chili powder, onion powder, one-half tablespoon crushed red pepper, beef bouillon crystals, chicken bouillon crystals, salt, and pepper. Stir, bring to boil, reduce heat, add enough water to cover, and let simmer for one hour. Add one tablespoon cumin and the remaining chili powder, stir, and simmer for another one-half hour. Add remaining red pepper, onion powder, and cumin and simmer for additional one-half hour. Serve with corn bread and iced tea.

Beginner's Chili #1

This simple recipe can be considered a starting point for the culinary-impaired, at least as it relates to chili. While yielding a socially acceptable bowl o' red (depending on which society you belong to), it should be abandoned at the first opportunity, with the enterprising chili cook moving on to more advanced recipes.

1   pound ground beef
1   medium onion, chopped
1   15-ounce can tomatoes
1   15-ounce can kidney beans
1   teaspoon salt
1   teaspoon pepper
1   tablespoon chili powder

Using a small amount of cooking oil, brown beef in cast-iron skillet, add onions, and drain if necessary. Add tomatoes, beans, salt, pepper, and chili powder. Stir well and let simmer for at least thirty minutes, adding water if necessary.

Beginner's Chili #2

Once you've mastered Beginner's Chili #1 and are ready for a bit more adventure, but you remain a touch too timid for the real thing, give this simple recipe a try. If you feel daring, add a bit more chili powder than the recipe calls for, perhaps an extra tablespoonful or two. The beans are optional.

1	tablespoon olive oil
1	onion, chopped
2	garlic cloves, minced
1	pound coarsely ground beef
2	tablespoons ground red pepper
¼	teaspoon cayenne pepper
1	teaspoon cumin

Salt to taste

1	16-ounce can tomatoes
3	cups water
2	whole cloves
1	green bell pepper, chopped
1	can pinto beans

Heat oil in large cast-iron skillet, add onion and garlic, and sauté. Add meat and cook until browned. Add remaining ingredients, except for beans, bring to boil, and let simmer for two to three hours, stirring occasionally. Add beans, and continue to simmer for another thirty minutes. Adjust seasoning to taste.

Black Coffee Chili

A *number of chiliheads are convinced that a dose of strong, black coffee in a pot of chili adds dimension to the flavor. This recipe not only includes the added taste dimension of coffee, but also that of beer!*

2	tablespoons canola oil
3	large onions, chopped
4	garlic cloves, minced
4-5	tablespoons chili powder
1	teaspoon cayenne pepper
1	tablespoon cumin
2	teaspoons paprika
2	pounds lean beef, cubed
1	12-ounce bottle of Mexican beer
½	cup black coffee, espresso desirable
½	cup fresh parsley, chopped
½	cup tomato paste

In a large cast-iron skillet, heat oil, add onions and garlic, and sauté. Add chili powder, cayenne, cumin, and paprika, stir, and cook for another two minutes. Add meat, stir, and brown. Add beer, coffee, parsley, and tomato paste, stir well; reduce heat, and allow to simmer for at least one hour or until meat is tender. Add water or beer when liquid is needed. Adjust for seasonings and serve.

Black Coffee Chili #2

Here is another chili recipe that incorporates black coffee as an ingredient.

3 dried ancho chile peppers, stemmed, seeded, and peeled

2 dried chipotle chile peppers, stemmed, seeded, and peeled

3 tablespoons olive oil

2 pounds lean beef, trimmed and cubed

2 medium onions, chopped

3 garlic cloves, minced

2 cans beef broth

1 cup strong black coffee

1 teaspoon oregano

1 teaspoon cumin

1 small can tomato paste

Salt and pepper to taste

Place ancho and chipotle chile peppers in a shallow bowl, cover with boiling water, and allow to set for at least thirty minutes. Heat oil in large cast-iron skillet and brown beef. Remove and pat dry. In the same skillet, sauté onions and garlic, and set aside. Place chile peppers in a blender along with one cup of water and puree. Place puree, along with broth, in a cooking pot. Add beef, onions, garlic, and more liquid, if necessary, to cover. Bring to boil, reduce heat, and simmer for one hour. Add coffee, oregano, cumin, tomato paste, salt, and pepper and simmer for another two hours, adding liquid if needed and adjusting for taste.

Blanco County Chili

This recipe, according to several Blanco County, Texas, residents, was a favorite of the late President Lyndon B. Johnson.

2 tablespoons cooking oil
4 pounds beef, coarsely ground
1 large onion, chopped
2 garlic cloves, minced
6-8 tablespoons chili powder
1 teaspoon oregano
1 teaspoon cumin
1 16-ounce can tomatoes
2 cups water
Salt to taste

In a large cooking pot, heat oil and brown beef. Add onion and garlic and sauté. Add the rest of the ingredients, bring to boil, cover, lower heat, and simmer for at least one hour, stirring and tasting occasionally.

Bob's Drunken Chili

I've had this recipe for so long that I have forgotten who Bob was. Though it has been modified over the years, the essential ingredients remain the same and have always yielded a magnificent bowl of chili.

2   tablespoons olive oil
6   fresh chile peppers, stemmed, seeded, and chopped (Use Anaheim, ancho, New Mexico, or jalapeño, or any combination)
1   onion, chopped
2   garlic cloves, minced
2   pounds lean beef, trimmed and cubed
1   bottle dark Mexican beer
1   can beef broth
1   teaspoon cumin
1   teaspoon paprika
1   teaspoon oregano
Salt and pepper to taste

After trimming the beef, give the fat to the dog. Heat oil in a cooking pot, add chile peppers, onion, garlic, and sauté. Add beef and cook until brown, stirring often. Add beer and broth, bring to boil, reduce heat, and simmer for one-half hour. Add cumin, paprika, oregano, salt, and pepper, stir, and simmer for an additional hour. Stir frequently during the simmering process, adjusting for taste.

Bobby Jack's Garlic Chili

This chili recipe was provided by Bobby Jack Childress, one of the finest Panhandle cowhands who ever straddled a horse, rounded up a cow, strung a barbed wire fence, or repaired a broken windmill. His recipe calls for considerably more garlic than most and yields a strikingly delicious bowl o' red. When I dined on Bobby Jack's chili I could never stop until I consumed at least three bowls.

1	tablespoon oregano
1	tablespoon paprika
5	tablespoon chili powder
1	tablespoon cumin
1	teaspoon instant beef bouillon
1	bottle dark Mexican beer
1	cup beef broth
3	tablespoons olive oil
2½	pounds beef chuck, trimmed and cubed
1	large onion, chopped
4	garlic cloves, minced
1	teaspoon Tabasco sauce
1	8-ounce can tomato sauce

Salt and pepper to taste

In a large cooking pot, add oregano, paprika, chili powder, cumin, bouillon, beer, and broth. Stir, bring to boil, reduce heat, and let simmer. In a large cast-iron skillet, heat oil and brown beef. Remove, pat dry, and add to pot. Add more oil to the skillet if necessary, toss in the onion and garlic, and sauté. Add to pot. If more liquid is needed, add more broth or water. Simmer for additional two hours. Add Tabasco sauce, tomato sauce, salt, and pepper, stir, and simmer for another thirty minutes. If a thicker chili is desired, mix a paste of water and masa harina and add one or two tablespoons. If a thinner chili is needed, simply add more water.

Brisket Chili

Brisket, not a traditional cut of meat used in chili, is effectively employed in this recipe.

2 tablespoons olive oil
3 pounds brisket, trimmed and cubed
1 large onion, chopped
3 garlic cloves, minced
Salt and pepper to taste
1 8-ounce can tomato sauce
1 cup beef broth
1 bottle dark Mexican beer
6 tablespoons chili powder
2 tablespoons cumin
1 teaspoon oregano
1 teaspoon Tabasco sauce
2 fresh jalapeño pepper, minced

In a large cooking pot, heat oil and brown brisket. Add onion and garlic and sauté. Add salt, pepper, tomato sauce, broth, beer, chili powder, cumin, oregano, and Tabasco sauce; stir, bring to boil, reduce heat, and simmer for at least three hours. Check for liquid and add water if necessary. Fifteen minutes before chili is to be served, add jalapeño peppers. Serve topped with freshly chopped cilantro.

Bunkhouse Chili

This is an easy-to-follow, inexpensive recipe for some fine-tasting chili. I first sampled this recipe one cold winter afternoon while working at the Hueco Mountain Ranch.

2	tablespoons bacon grease
2	pounds coarsely ground chuck
1	large onion, chopped
1	8-ounce can tomato sauce
2	teaspoons garlic powder
5	tablespoons chili powder
1	tablespoon cumin
1	teaspoon oregano
1	teaspoon cayenne pepper

Salt and pepper to taste

1	teaspoon Tabasco sauce
1	bottle dark Mexican beer
2	fresh jalapeño chile peppers, minced

In a cooking pot heat bacon grease and brown meat. Add onion and sauté. Add tomato sauce and garlic powder, bring to boil, reduce heat, and simmer for one-half hour. Add chili powder, cumin, oregano, cayenne pepper, salt, pepper, Tabasco sauce, and beer, stir, and continue to simmer for another hour. Fifteen minutes before serving, stir in the minced jalapeño peppers. Serve with a side of pinto beans and fresh corn bread.

Chili a la Frontera

Frontera means border in Spanish, and this version owes a debt to the Mexican influence on cooking at and near the Texas-Mexico border. Chorizo, one of the principle ingredients, is a Mexican sausage rich in spices and taste.

3	tomatoes, peeled
1-2	large onions, chopped
¼	teaspoon oregano
1-2	teaspoons paprika
3-4	garlic cloves, minced
4	pounds lean beef, coarsely ground
1	pound chorizo, chopped
1-2	tablespoons bacon drippings
20	scallions, chopped
3-4	green bell peppers, chopped
5	hot chile peppers (jalapeño or serrano)
6-8	tablespoons chili powder
1	tablespoon cumin
1-2	bottles dark Mexican beer
Salt to taste	

Mash tomatoes, onions, oregano, paprika, and one clove of garlic together in a bowl. Place mixture in a large cooking pot along with beef. Heat bacon drippings in cast-iron skillet, add scallions, bell peppers, chile peppers, the remaining garlic, and chorizo and cook over low to medium heat until sausage is browned. Add to pot with mashed vegetables and meat; stir well, add salt, chili powder, cumin, and enough beer to cover. Bring to boil, lower heat, and simmer for three to four hours or until beef is tender. Adjust seasonings to taste.

Chili Con Chorizo

This is another chili recipe employing chorizo, the spicy Mexican-style sausage commonly found in supermarkets and restaurants throughout much of Texas and the Southwest. For an interesting change, try this delightfully tasty recipe.

1 pound chorizo, chopped
1 pound pork loin, finely cubed
2 medium onions, chopped
3 garlic cloves, minced
1 red bell pepper, chopped
3 tablespoons chili powder
1 tablespoon oregano
1 tablespoon cumin
1 teaspoon cayenne pepper
1 14½-ounce can crushed tomatoes

In a large cooking pot, cook chorizo over medium heat until done. Add pork loin, onions, garlic, and red pepper and cook for another ten minutes or until pork is browned. Drain. Add chili powder, oregano, cumin, and cayenne, stir well, and cook for another minute or two. Add tomatoes, mix well, reduce heat, and simmer for thirty to forty-five minutes. Serve with a side of beans or rice and a couple of fresh corn tortillas.

Chili Parlor Chili

This recipe was found in a trunk full of papers, menus, and bills saved from an old-time Dallas chili parlor that operated during the 1930s. The recipe calls for what seems like a lot of cumin seeds and chile, but maybe they liked their chili well-seasoned in thoses days.

¼   cup bacon grease
2   pounds lean beef, coarsely ground
1   cup cumin seeds
1   cup dried and ground New Mexico red chiles
¼   teaspoon cayenne
2   garlic cloves, minced
Salt and pepper to taste
1   teaspoon paprika

Heat bacon grease in a large cast-iron skillet, add meat, and cook for approximately eight to ten minutes or until brown. Stir in cumin seeds and ground red chile, reduce heat, and let simmer for one-half hour. Add water if needed. Add cayenne and garlic, stir, and simmer for additional two hours. Add salt, pepper, and paprika, stirring it into the mix. If a thicker chili is desired, mix two tablespoons of masa harina with two tablespoons bacon grease and dump it into the pot. Serve with saltines.

Chorizo Chili

Similar to previous recipes using chorizo, this is a favorite dish commonly encountered in the Texas and New Mexico Southwest. The use of chorizo, a Mexican sausage, adds a pleasing dimension. The addition of celery in this recipe, though not a common ingredient, compliments the pork and chorizo nicely.

3   tablespoons olive oil
2   pounds pork, trimmed and cubed
2   onions, chopped
3   garlic cloves, minced
1   stalk celery, chopped
1   can beef broth
2   teaspoons cumin
2   teaspoons oregano
6   dried Anaheim chiles, stemmed, seeded, and chopped
Salt to taste
½   pound chorizo

Place dried chiles in a bowl and cover with boiling water, stir, and set aside for at least one-half hour. Heat half of the olive oil in a skillet, add pork, and brown. Remove meat and set aside, and wipe skillet clean. Heat remaining oil and sauté onions, garlic, and celery. Place pork and vegetables in a cooking pot and cover with broth, adding water if necessary. Bring to boil, add cumin, oregano, and salt, stir, reduce heat, and simmer for two hours. Place reconstituted chiles in blender and puree. Remove skins by straining through sieve or colander. Place puree in chili and stir. After chili has simmered for approximately one hour, break chorizo into skillet and cook until done. Drain grease, pat meat dry, and add to chili, and stir. Check the chili from time to time, adding water and seasonings as needed.

Competition Chili

*T*his recipe has been adapted from three or four cook-off-winning chilis. Since cook-off competitions generally use diced meat and forbid the presence of visible vegetables, commercially available powdered and minced onion and garlic are employed for a prize winning chili for friends and family.

2   tablespoons olive oil
3   pounds coarse-ground beef
1   cup beef broth
2   teaspoons beef bouillon crystals
1   teaspoon chicken bouillon crystals
1   8-ounce can tomato sauce
3   tablespoons minced onion
2   teaspoons garlic powder
8   tablespoons chili powder
2   teaspoons Tabasco sauce
Salt and pepper to taste
1   teaspoon onion powder
1½   tablespoons cumin
1   tablespoon paprika
2   teaspoons crushed red pepper

In a large cooking pot, heat olive oil, add meat, and cook until brown. Add broth, beef bouillon and chicken bouillon crystals, tomato sauce, minced onion, one teaspoon garlic powder, two tablespoons chili powder, and Tabasco sauce. Stir, bring to boil, reduce heat, and let simmer for one hour. Add salt and pepper, onion powder, the remaining garlic powder, one tablespoon cumin, paprika, the remaining chili powder, and one teaspoon of crushed red pepper. Stir and simmer for another hour. Add remaining cumin and red pepper, stir, and cook for an additional thirty minutes.

Crockpot Chili for Novices

This recipe, like the one for Beginner's Chili, is designed for newcomers to the world of chili, for the faint of heart, or for those with tender stomachs. Once this simple dish is mastered and a desire for better things is evident, move on to some of the more advanced recipes.

2½ pounds beef stew meat, cubed
1 15½-ounce can kidney beans, drained
1 15½-ounce can Great Northern beans, drained
2 14½-ounce cans seasoned diced tomatoes
1 large onion, chopped
1 teaspoon salt
1 teaspoon pepper
1 16-ounce jar salsa
4 teaspoons chili powder

Combine beef, beans, tomatoes, onion, salt, and pepper in a crock pot, mix well, cover, and cook on low setting for eight to nine hours or until beef is tender. When done, place in large cast-iron skillet, add salsa and chili powder, and heat for five to ten minutes, stirring often.

Crockpot Chili for Novices #2

The use of sugar and bell pepper in this recipe suggests it had it origins in the American South.

1	pound ground round
1	cup chopped onion
½	cup chopped bell pepper
¼	cup red wine
1	tablespoon chili powder
1	teaspoon sugar
1	teaspoon cumin
¼	teaspoon salt
1	garlic clove, minced
1	15-ounce can kidney beans
1	14½-ounce can spiced stewed tomatoes
6	tablespoons cheddar cheese, shredded

Brown meat in skillet, add onions, bell pepper, wine, chili powder, sugar, cumin, salt, and garlic and continue to cook until onion is tender. Place mixture in crock pot, add beans and tomatoes, and stir well. Cover and cook on low heat for four hours. After spooning chili into bowls, sprinkle top with shredded cheese.

Dallas County Jailhouse Chili

This tried and true recipe has been a favorite with Texans for decades. It is also very easy to prepare.

2	cups beef suet
2	pounds coarsely ground beef
3	garlic buds, minced
1½	tablespoons paprika
3	tablespoons chili powder
1	tablespoon cumin
1	tablespoon salt
1	teaspoon white pepper
1½	sweet chili pods, chopped fine
3	cups water

Fry suet in cast-iron skillet. Add meat, garlic, and remaining seasonings, cover, and simmer for four hours, stirring occasionally. Add water as needed and cook for another hour until slightly thickened.

Chili DeGolyer

E. *DeGolyer, as described by H. Allen Smith, was "a world traveler, a gourmet, a litterateur, a sense-making citizen of Dallas, and a gentleman." DeGolyer invested a lot of time studying chili history and lore and worked for years to arrive at the following recipe. DeGolyer owned the* Saturday Review of Literature, *and Smith referred to him as "the Solomon of the chili bowl."*

2½ cups fat rendered from beef suet

1 onion, chopped

3 pounds center cut steak, cut into ½-inch cubes

2 cups water

2-12 pods of dried red chiles (Adjust amount to taste. May substitute one tablespoon chili powder for each two pods of chile)

4 cloves garlic, finely chopped

1 teaspoon cumin

1 teaspoon oregano

1 tablespoon salt

Heat fat in a large skillet, add onion and sauté. Add meat and cook until gray. Add water and let simmer for one hour. While meat is simmering, wash chiles and remove stems and seeds. In a separate pot, boil chiles until skins come off (one-half to three-quarters of an hour). Press chiles through a colander to form a paste. Add chiles, cumin, oregano, and salt to the meat and cook for another hour.

Expedition Chili

As an avid backpacker who spends several days at a time in remote, mountainous regions, I have long ago grown tired of the commercially packaged freeze-dried foods, all of which seem to taste the same, which is to say like cardboard. There is no rule that says one has to dine on bland, tasteless food in the wilderness, so I devised the following recipe for Expedition Chili. All of the ingredients are light and easy to carry and don't add significant weight to one's pack. The garlic powder, onion powder, chili powder, cumin, and oregano can be mixed well ahead of time and carried in a small plastic bag. This recipe also works well in hunting camp or on family campouts.

8   ounces beef jerky
2   cups water
1   tablespoon garlic powder
1   tablespoon onion powder
1   teaspoon cumin
1   teaspoon oregano
3   tablespoons chili powder
Salt to taste

Cut jerky into three-quarter-inch pieces and place in cooking pot. Add water and bring to boil. Add garlic powder, onion powder, cumin, oregano, chili powder, and salt, reduce heat, and let simmer for two hours, adjusting for seasonings and liquid.

Fajita Chili

The Spanish word fajita means skirt and initially referred to a cut of meat known as the skirt steak, or flank steak. The Tex-Mex dish called fajitas is traditionally made from flank steak, as is this style of chili, which is commonly found along the Texas-Mexico border.

2   tablespoons cooking oil

2   pounds flank steak, cubed

Salt and pepper to taste

4   dried ancho chiles, roasted, peeled, stemmed, and seeded

3   cups beef broth

4   garlic cloves, minced

2   tablespoons oregano

1   tablespoon cumin

6   fresh Anaheim chiles, chopped

1   jalapeño chile, chopped

4   onions, chopped

In a cast-iron skillet, heat oil, drop in meat, and brown. Salt and pepper meat as it cooks. Place dried anchos in a blender along with two cups beef broth and puree. Place meat in a cooking pot. Add onions and garlic to skillet and sauté. Add to meat, stir, and cook for a few minutes. Add ancho puree, oregano, cumin, fresh Anaheim chiles, and jalapeño chile; stir again, and continue cooking. Add more beef broth for liquid. Reduce heat and allow to simmer for two hours or until flank steak is tender enough to pull apart with a fork. Adjust for seasoning.

Goat Chili

Cabrito, or goat, is commonly raised and eaten in Mexico and in parts of the American Southwest. It was only a matter of time before goat meat was employed in the making of chili. This recipe comes from an American Indian community in northern New Mexico.

2 tablespoons cooking oil

2 pounds goat meat, trimmed and cubed

2 medium onions, chopped

3 cloves garlic, minced

2 jalapeño chile peppers, chopped

1 bottle dark Mexican beer

1 8-ounce can tomato sauce

6 New Mexico chile peppers, stemmed, seeded, and peeled, and chopped

3 tablespoons chili powder

2 teaspoons oregano

1 teaspoon cumin

1 teaspoon paprika

Salt and pepper to taste

For best results, soak goat meat in milk overnight. In a cast-iron skillet, heat oil, brown the goat meat, and transfer to a cooking pot. Using a bit more oil, sauté onions, garlic, and jalapeños. When done, add to meat in the pot and cover with beer and tomato sauce. If more liquid is needed, add water. Bring to a boil, reduce heat, and simmer for two hours. As soon as simmering begins, place New Mexico chiles in a blender, puree until a pasty consistency is reached, and add to pot. Add chili powder, oregano, cumin, paprika, salt, and pepper, and stir. Serve with fresh corn tortillas and top with freshly chopped cilantro.

Gold Rush Chili

The following was adapted from and improved over what is purported to be an original recipe followed by some forty-niners passing through Texas on their way west to the California gold fields.

1   large onion, chopped
6   garlic cloves, minced
2   cups chicken broth
2   tablespoons bacon grease
3   pounds lean beef, trimmed and cubed
½   cup tomato sauce
5   tablespoons powdered California chile peppers
4   tablespoons powdered New Mexico chile peppers
1   tablespoon powdered ancho chile peppers
Salt to taste
1   teaspoon cayenne pepper
1   teaspoon Tabasco sauce

In a large cooking pot, simmer the onion and garlic in chicken broth for ten minutes. In a large cast-iron skillet, heat bacon grease and brown meat. Add meat to vegetables and broth, along with tomato sauce, powdered chiles, salt, and cayenne pepper. Stir, bring to boil, cover pot, reduce heat, and let simmer for two hours. Add liquid (water or broth) if necessary, adjust for seasoning. Add Tabasco sauce fifteen minutes before serving. Top with chopped fresh parsley.

Green Chile and Pork Chili

This is yet another recipe from the New Mexico Southwest and one that is commonly found served in the homes of Indians and Mexicans.

3   pounds pork shoulder, boned and cubed
⅓   cup flour
3   onions, chopped
3   cloves garlic, minced
2   16-ounce cans green chiles, cut into strips
2   16-ounce cans tomatoes
1   6-ounce can tomato paste
3   cups water
½   teaspoon oregano
Salt to taste

Remove fat from pork and melt it in a cast-iron skillet. After coating the meat with flour, add to skillet, brown, and place in large pot, preferably a Dutch oven. Place onions and garlic in skillet and sauté. When done, add to the meat. Stir remaining ingredients into the pot, bring to boil, reduce heat, then simmer for forty-five minutes. Taste and adjust for seasonings, simmer another one-half hour, and serve with Navajo fry bread.

Gulf Coast Chili

According to some of our friends who live in the Texas Gulf Coast city of Galveston, this recipe was arrived at after some seven years of experimenting. They promise the result is sure to please any serious chili aficionado. Be sure to make enough for seconds.

2	tablespoons olive oil
2	pounds beef chuck, cubed
6	tablespoons chili powder
2	tablespoons minced garlic
1	teaspoon jalapeño powder
1	8-ounce can tomato sauce
1	cup beef broth
1½	tablespoons onion powder
1½	tablespoons garlic powder
1	teaspoon crushed red pepper
Salt to taste	
2	fresh jalapeño peppers, minced
1	tablespoon paprika
1	bottle dark Mexican beer (optional)

In a large cooking pot, heat oil and add beef. As the meat is browning, add one tablespoon chili powder and one tablespoon minced garlic. Add jalapeño powder, tomato sauce, beef broth, onion powder, garlic powder, and red pepper, two tablespoons chili powder, and salt. Stir, bring to boil, reduce heat, and allow to simmer for one-and-a-half hours. If additional liquid is needed, add beef broth. Add jalapeño peppers, paprika, the remaining chili powder, onion powder, and garlic powder; stir and simmer for another one-half hour. Check for liquid and add beer, broth, or water if necessary. Adjust for seasoning and serve.

Habanero Beef Chili

*C*aution! *Habanero peppers are considered to be the hottest on earth. In spite of that, they are also incredibly tasty. If you tend to be sensitive to extremely hot chiles, reduce the amount. If, on the other hand, you crave the heat of incendiary peppers, add an extra habanero. Keep a glass of iced water, tea, or milk close by. And by the way, be sure to wear some rubber gloves while working with the habaneros and refrain from touching exposed skin.*

2 tablespoons olive oil
2 pounds lean beef, trimmed and cubed
2 medium onions, chopped
3 cloves garlic, minced
1 stalk celery, chopped
2 habanero chile peppers, finely chopped
1 bottle dark Mexican beer
1 teaspoon cumin
Salt to taste

In a large cast-iron skillet, heat oil, add meat, and brown. Add onions, garlic, celery, and habaneros, and sauté. Add beer, stir, and cook for another ten minutes. Add cumin and salt, stir, bring to boil, reduce heat, and allow to simmer for one-and-a-half hours. If a thinner chili is desired, add more beer or water. If a thicker chili is desired, mix a paste of masa harina and water and add. Top with chopped cilantro.

2 lbs. beef.
@ 1 onion, 1T cumin, 2t coriander, 2t oregano,
½ of a 15oz can tomato sauce,
no celery, 1 bottle beer
2 habaneros   vs.   6 jalapeños

Habanero Chicken Chili

Since I have been growing habaneros for the past several years, I have been searching for a variety of ways in which to incorporate these fiery yet oh-so-tasty peppers into a variety of dishes. In the process of experimenting, I have discovered that habanero peppers and chicken go together very well.

4   ancho chile peppers, dried, peeled, stemmed, and seeded
2   tablespoons olive oil
2   medium onions, chopped
3   garlic cloves, minced
2   cups chicken broth
1-2 dried ground habanero chile peppers (according to taste and tolerance)
1   teaspoon rosemary
1   teaspoon cumin
3-4 pounds chicken, cut into sections
Salt and pepper to taste

After slicing ancho peppers in half, place in shallow bowl, cover with boiling water, and let soak for at least thirty minutes. When anchos have been rehydrated, place in blender with small amount of water, puree, and set aside. Heat oil in cooking pot and sauté onions and garlic. Add puree, chicken broth, habaneros, rosemary, cumin, chicken, salt, and pepper. Stir, bring to boil, reduce heat, and simmer for one hour. Turn off heat and allow pot to cool. Remove chicken sections, remove meat from bones, discard bones, and chop meat. Return meat to pot and cook for another one-half hour. Serve with chopped fresh parsley or cilantro and a squeeze of fresh lime.

High Plains Chili

The high plains and Panhandle country of Texas is the source for this recipe.

4   slices bacon
2   onions, chopped
1   clove garlic, minced
1   pound lean round steak, cubed
½   pound chuck steak, cubed
½   pound pork shoulder, cubed
2   cans chopped green chiles
2   tablespoons chili powder
1   teaspoon Mexican oregano
1   teaspoon cumin
Salt to taste
2   6-ounce cans tomato paste
2-3 cups water
1   16-ounce can pinto beans

Fry bacon to medium crispiness in large cast-iron skillet, remove, place on paper towel, and save the grease. Place onions and garlic into skillet and sauté until onions are translucent. Add beef and pork to skillet and cook until browned, stirring occasionally. Add green chiles, chili powder, oregano, cumin, salt, and tomato paste. Bring to boil, then reduce heat and simmer for about two hours or until meat is tender and easily cut with a fork. When ready to serve, add beans and bacon, simmer for another fifteen to twenty minutes, and serve.

Hill Country Chili

This recipe was adapted from one we found at the home of a friend in Kerrville, Texas. While it calls for beef, we have found it works equally well with pork. Chili powder, red pepper, and jalapeño powder provide for a fiery bowl of delicious red, so keep a glass of something cool and wet nearby.

3 tablespoons olive oil
3 pounds lean chuck, trimmed and cubed
1 8-ounce can tomato sauce
2 cans beef broth
2 teaspoons beef bouillon
2 tablespoons minced onion
6 tablespoons chili powder
2 teaspoon crushed red pepper
1 teaspoon jalapeño powder
Black pepper to taste, not to exceed 1 teaspoon
1 tablespoon minced garlic
½ teaspoon white pepper
2 tablespoons cumin
Salt to taste

Heat oil in large cooking pot and brown beef. Add tomato sauce and enough broth to cover meat, bring to boil, reduce heat, add beef bouillon, one tablespoon minced onion, three tablespoons chili powder, one teaspoon red pepper, and jalapeño powder, stir, and allow to simmer for one hour. Add black pepper, the remaining minced onion, minced garlic, white pepper, one tablespoon cumin, the remaining chili powder, and salt. Stir and simmer for one-half hour. Add remaining cumin, remaining red pepper, stir, and let simmer for another hour. Adjust for taste. If liquid is needed, add beef broth.

Hotter Than a Smokin' Pistol Chili

This is a peppered-up version of traditional Texas chili that will lift the hat right off your head. The use of jalapeño, pasilla, Anaheim, and arbol chiles provides for a volatile concoction, but one that is incredibly tasty.

3	tablespoons olive oil
2	pounds lean beef, trimmed and cubed
1	large onion, chopped
2	garlic cloves, minced
1	bottle dark Mexican beer
1	can beef broth
3	fresh jalapeño chile peppers, stemmed and finely chopped
1	tablespoon pasilla chile powder
1	tablespoon Anaheim chile powder
1	teaspoon chile arbol powder
2	teaspoons cumin
2	teaspoons oregano

Salt to taste

Heat oil in a cast-iron skillet and brown the beef. Remove meat and set aside, then sauté onions and garlic, adding more oil if necessary. Place meat and vegetables in a cooking pot, and add beer and broth. Bring to boil, add jalapeños, pasilla powder, Anaheim powder, arbol powder, cumin, oregano, and salt. Stir, reduce heat, and simmer for two hours or until meat is tender. If more liquid is needed, add more beer or broth according to taste. If a thicker chili is desired, add a bit of paste made from masa harina and water. Top with freshly chopped cilantro.

Jalapeño Chili

If you like fiery chili but cannot endure the intense heat of habaneros, try this dish made with the equally tasty but somewhat less hellish jalapeños.

3	tablespoons olive oil
2	pounds lean beef, trimmed and cubed
1	large onion, chopped
2	garlic cloves, minced
6	jalapeño chile peppers, stemmed and finely chopped
2	cups beef broth
1	8-ounce can tomato sauce
2	tablespoons chili powder
1	teaspoon cumin
1	teaspoon oregano

Salt to taste

Heat two tablespoons olive oil in a cast-iron skillet and brown meat. Remove meat, discard grease, and wipe pan clean. Add remaining tablespoon of olive oil and sauté onion, garlic, and jalapeño peppers. Place meat and sautéed vegetables in a cooking pot, add broth, tomato sauce, chili powder, cumin, oregano, and salt, and stir. If liquid is needed to cover the chili, add water. Bring to boil, reduce heat, and let simmer for one-and-a-half hours or until meat is tender. Adjust for seasoning and add water if necessary.

Leftover Thanksgiving Turkey Chili

Tired of turkey sandwiches for days after Thanksgiving? Here is an excellent and pleasing way to transform leftover holiday turkey into a delightful chili.

4 dried Anaheim chiles, stemmed, seeded, and chopped

2 tablespoons olive oil

1½-2 pounds leftover turkey, chopped

1 large onion, chopped

2 garlic cloves, minced

1 stalk celery, chopped

2 cups chicken broth

1 8-ounce can tomato sauce

1 teaspoon cumin

1 teaspoon oregano

Salt and pepper to taste

Place dried chiles in bowl, add boiling water, stir, and allow to set for one-half hour. Heat one tablespoon olive oil in skillet and brown turkey. Drain, remove from skillet, and pat dry. Wipe pan clean with a paper towel and add remaining oil, heat, and sauté onion, garlic, and celery. Place turkey and vegetables in a cooking pot, add broth, tomato sauce, cumin, oregano, salt, and pepper. Stir, bring to boil, and reduce heat to simmer. Place dried chiles in a blender and puree until a paste is formed. Remove skins by straining, add the puree to chili, and stir. Allow to cook for at least an hour, adjusting for liquids and seasonings as needed.

Luna County Chili

I *first tasted this recipe while visiting a rancher in Luna County, New Mexico. It reminded me of a cross between chili and posole, a delicious hominy-based Mexican stew. It was cold and windy that evening as we dined, but the chili warmed our bodies and souls.*

6   dried New Mexico red chile peppers, stemmed, seeded, and peeled

2   dried chipotle chile peppers, stemmed, seeded, and peeled

2   tablespoons olive oil

2   pounds lean beef, trimmed and cubed

2   medium onions, chopped

3   garlic cloves, minced

1   teaspoon cumin

1   teaspoon oregano

Salt and pepper to taste

2   10-ounce cans beef broth

1   16-ounce can hominy

Slice New Mexico and chipotle chile peppers in half and place in shallow bowl, cover with boiling water, and allow to set for at least thirty minutes. In a large cast-iron skillet, heat oil and brown meat, drain, pat dry, and set aside. In the same skillet, sauté onions and garlic, adding more oil if necessary. Drain, remove, and set aside. Place New Mexico reds and chipotles in a blender and puree. Place puree in cooking pot and add cumin, oregano, salt, and pepper. Cover with beef broth, stir, and bring to boil. Add onions and garlic, beef, and hominy, reduce heat, and let simmer over low heat for three hours. Top with fresh chopped cilantro.

New Mexico Red

With the proliferation of chile farms throughout much of New Mexico, the chances for finding some excellent bowls of chili are getting better and better. This recipe for the ever-popular New Mexico red is encountered mostly in the southeastern part of the Land of Enchantment close to the Texas border.

2 tablespoons bacon grease
1 large onion, chopped
3 pounds sirloin, cubed
3 garlic cloves, minced
4 tablespoons red chile, ground
2 tablespoons paprika
2 teaspoons ground cumin
3 cups water
Salt and pepper to taste

Heat bacon grease in a cast-iron skillet, add onion, and sauté until golden brown. Add meat, garlic, chile, paprika, and cumin and stir well until meat is browned. Add water, salt, and pepper, bring to boil, then simmer for two to three hours, stirring occasionally. Taste the concoction from time to time and add more seasonings if desired. Add water as needed.

New Mexico Red #2

This simple and easy-to-prepare version of New Mexico red chili was adapted from a recipe commonly used by American Indians residing in the northern part of the state. Interestingly, this recipe does not call for New Mexico red chiles.

15-20 Anaheim chiles, dried, roasted, peeled, stemmed, and seeded
5 garlic cloves, minced
5 cups beef broth
2 tablespoons lard
2 pounds lean chuck, cubed
Salt and pepper to taste
1 tablespoon cumin
1 tablespoon oregano

In a blender, puree dried chiles along with garlic and two cups beef broth. In a large cooking pot, heat lard, add beef, and brown, salting and peppering the meat as it cooks. Drain and add chile puree, cumin, and oregano; stir, and cook for another two to three minutes. Add more beef broth to desired level; stir, bring to boil, reduce heat, and simmer for two hours. Serve with a side dish of pinto beans and corn tortillas.

New Mexico Green

This simple-to-make, tasty, somewhat nontraditional dish is made with pork and green chiles instead of beef and red chiles. Commonly found on Indian reservations in New Mexico, it offers a nice variation on the usual pot of chili.

2	tablespoons cooking oil
2-2½	pounds pork loin, cubed
	Salt and pepper to taste
1	large onion, chopped
4-5	garlic cloves, minced
15-20	fresh green Anaheim chiles, roasted, peeled, and stemmed
2-3	cups chicken broth

In a cooking pot, heat cooking oil and brown the pork, salting and peppering it as it cooks. Drain. Add onion and garlic and sauté. When onions are translucent, add chiles and chicken broth, bring to boil, reduce heat, and allow to simmer for one hour. Adjust for seasoning. Serve over rice or with a side of pinto beans and corn bread or corn tortillas, and garnish with chopped green onions or fresh cilantro.

Jay Pennington's Chili

*J*ay Pennington won the eleventh annual International Chili Society's world championship in 1977 with the following recipe.

1	tablespoon cooking oil
3	medium onions, finely chopped
2	green bell peppers, finely chopped
2	stalks celery, finely chopped
3	cloves garlic, minced
8	pounds round steak, coarsely ground
5	cups tomato sauce
5	cups stewed tomatoes
5	cups water
1	6-ounce can tomato paste
1	4-ounce can salsa
1	can hot green peppers, finely chopped
6	ounces chili powder
1	4-ounce can chopped green chiles

Pinch of oregano
Salt, pepper, and garlic salt to taste

Heat oil in a ten- to twelve-quart pot, add onions, bell peppers, celery, and garlic and sauté until onions are translucent. Add meat, stirring occasionally until browned. Add remaining ingredients, mixing well. Bring to boil, lower heat, and simmer two-and-a-half to three hours, stirring occasionally. Adjust to taste.

Pedernales River Chili

A *tried and true chili recipe, considered a standard for most serious chili cooks, and reputed to be one of President Lyndon B. Johnson's favorites.*

3   tablespoons bacon drippings
4   pounds lean beef, coarsely ground
1   large onion, chopped
2   garlic cloves, minced
Salt to taste
1   teaspoon oregano
1   teaspoon cumin
2   cups boiling water
1   32-ounce can tomatoes
4   tablespoons ground red chile, hot
2   tablespoons ground red chile, mild

Using a large cast-iron skillet, brown meat in heated bacon drippings. Add onion and garlic and cook over low heat until onion is translucent. Slowly, and lovingly, add salt, oregano, cumin, water, and tomatoes, stirring as you go. Gradually add the ground chiles until you have reached a taste you are satisfied with. Bring this mixture to a hard boil, reduce heat to simmer, and leave for approximately one hour, stirring occasionally.

Pork and Red Pepper Chili

This dish represents an interesting and tasty alternative to beef chili.

2 tablespoons olive oil

3 pounds pork butt, cubed

1 large onion, chopped

3 garlic cloves, minced

3 cups chicken broth

5 tablespoons chili powder

2 teaspoons oregano

2 teaspoons crushed red pepper

Salt to taste

½ cup red wine

In a large cast-iron skillet, heat oil and brown pork. Remove from skillet, pat dry, and set aside. Add onion and garlic to skillet and sauté. Stir in one cup of chicken broth, stir, and simmer for ten minutes. Place pork and vegetables in a large cooking pot, add chili powder, oregano, red pepper, salt, the remaining broth, and red wine. Stir, bring to boil, reduce heat, and let simmer for one-and-a-half hours or until pork is tender. Top with chopped fresh parsley and serve with corn tortillas.

Pueblo Indian Chili

We have been told that this recipe is hundreds of years old and was introduced by the Indians to some of the earliest Spanish explorers to New Mexico.

3 tablespoons lard
2 pounds beef, cubed
½ cup flour
1 medium onion, chopped
2 cloves garlic, minced
5 tablespoons ground red chile, hot
2-3 tablespoons ground red chile, mild
½ teaspoon Mexican oregano
4 cups beef broth
Salt, pepper, and cumin to taste
2-3 cups cooked pinto beans

While lard is melting in cast-iron skillet, place cubed meat and flour in a paper bag and shake well to coat the meat. Place meat in skillet and, when brown, add onion and garlic. Continue to cook until onion is translucent. Lower heat and add chiles, stirring well. Add remaining seasonings and allow to simmer for one-and-a-half to two hours, stirring occasionally. When meat is tender, serve, adding pinto beans as a side dish.

Red River Chili

From the Texas-Oklahoma border comes this favorite recipe.

2 tablespoons olive oil
2 pounds lean meat, trimmed and cubed
1 can beef broth
2 tablespoons minced onion
2 tablespoons minced garlic
2 teaspoons beef bouillon crystals
2 teaspoons chicken bouillon crystals
1 teaspoon cayenne
½ teaspoon white pepper
2 teaspoons paprika
Salt to taste
1 8-ounce can tomato sauce
5 tablespoons chili powder
2 tablespoons cumin
1 teaspoon crushed red pepper

In a large cooking pot, heat oil and brown meat. Add broth, one tablespoon minced onion, one tablespoon minced garlic, beef and chicken bouillon crystals, cayenne, white pepper, paprika, salt, and tomato sauce. Stir, reduce heat, and simmer for one hour. Add chili powder and cumin and simmer for another thirty minutes. Add remaining minced onion and garlic and red pepper, stir, and continue to simmer for additional thirty minutes. Adjust for seasoning and if more liquid is needed, add water.

Reno Red

This recipe won the thirteenth annual International Chili Society World Championship cook-off for Joe and Shirley Stewart in 1979.

3 pounds round steak, coarsely ground
3 pounds chuck steak, coarsely ground
1 cup cooking oil
Black pepper to taste
¾ cup chili powder, mild
6 tablespoons cumin
6 small gloves garlic, minced
2 medium onions, chopped
2 tablespoons MSG
6 dried New Mexico chile pods, seeded, stemmed, skinned, and boiled
1 tablespoon oregano, brewed like tea in ½ cup of beer
2 tablespoons paprika
2 tablespoons cider vinegar
3 cups beef broth
1 4-ounce can chopped green chiles
1 cup stewed tomatoes
1 teaspoon Tabasco sauce
2 tablespoons masa harina

In large pot, brown beef in oil, drain, and add pepper, chili powder, cumin, garlic, onions, and MSG. (While the Stewarts included MSG in their recipe, many chili cooks prefer to leave it out. Suit yourself.) Simmer for thirty to forty-five minutes, stirring often and adding water if needed. After pulping the chile pods, add to the mixture. Strain the oregano and beer mixture through a fine sieve and add the beer to the pot along with paprika, vinegar, two cups broth, green chiles, tomatoes, and Tabasco. Simmer another forty-five minutes, stirring occasionally. Mix masa into remaining broth, add to chili, and simmer for an additional thirty minutes.

Rio Grande Frontera Chili

The region around the Texas-Mexico border is where we encountered this recipe. It's good and spicy-hot, so you better keep a glass of milk or iced tea close by in case you need to put out a fire.

2   tablespoons olive oil
2   pounds coarsely ground chuck
1   14½-ounce can beef broth
1   14½-ounce can chicken broth
6   tablespoons chili powder
2   tablespoons garlic powder
2   teaspoons onion powder
1   teaspoon cayenne pepper
Salt and pepper to taste
1   tablespoon cumin
1   teaspoon oregano
1   can tomato sauce
Pinch of basil

Heat oil in a large cooking pot and brown meat. Add beef and chicken broth, three tablespoons chili powder, one tablespoon garlic powder, one teaspoon onion powder, and one-half teaspoon cayenne pepper. Stir, bring to boil, cover, and let simmer for one hour. Add remaining chili powder, garlic powder, onion powder, and cayenne pepper. Add more broth if liquid is needed, stir, and simmer for thirty minutes. Add tomato sauce and basil, stir, and simmer for another thirty minutes. Check for liquids and add broth if needed. Adjust for seasoning and serve topped with chopped fresh cilantro or parsley.

Sam's Southern Chili

This recipe is typical of many we encountered in the South and calls for lard, sugar, beans, and hamburger instead of chili grind or cubed meat.

2-3 tablespoons lard
1 large onion, chopped
4 pounds hamburger
6 tablespoons ground hot red chile
2 tablespoons ground mild red chile
2 tablespoons cumin
3 cloves garlic, minced
Salt to taste
Black pepper to taste
1 tablespoon sugar
1 12-ounce can tomatoes
3 16-ounce cans kidney beans

Melt lard in large cooking pot, add onion, and sauté. In a separate bowl, combine hamburger, ground chile, cumin, garlic, salt, and pepper, and add to pot, mixing well. Cook until hamburger is browned. Add remaining ingredients, stir well, and let simmer uncovered for two to three hours. Serve with corn bread and buttermilk.

Sausage Chili

Breakfast sausage is used to good advantage in this simple recipe.

2	cups onion, chopped
¾ - 1	pound breakfast sausage
2	cups water
1½	teaspoons chili powder
1½	teaspoons oregano, dried
1½	teaspoons cumin, ground
½	teaspoon salt
¼	teaspoon crushed red pepper
2	14½-ounce cans stewed tomatoes
1	15½-ounce can white beans
1	4½-ounce can chopped green chiles
2	cloves garlic, minced

Mix onion and sausage together in cast-iron pot and cook over medium heat until browned. Add water and remaining ingredients, stir well, bring to boil, reduce heat, and simmer for thirty minutes to an hour.

Sausage Chili #2

½ pound pork sausage

2 pounds pork roast, cubed

2 tablespoons olive oil

2 onions, chopped

3 garlic cloves, minced

1 8-ounce can tomato sauce

2 cups beef or chicken broth

4 fresh ancho chile peppers, stemmed, seeded, and chopped

2 jalapeño chile peppers, stemmed, seeded, and chopped

3 tablespoons chili powder

2 teaspoons cumin

2 teaspoon celery salt

2 teaspoons oregano

Salt and pepper to taste

Break up sausage in cast-iron skillet and lightly brown. Drain grease, add pork, and continue to cook until pork is browned. Remove meat and set aside. Heat olive oil in skillet, add onions and garlic, and sauté. Place sautéed vegetables in cooking pot, add meat, tomato sauce, and broth. Bring to boil, reduce heat, and simmer for one-and-a-half hours. As chili begins to simmer, place chile peppers in a blender and puree until a paste is formed. Remove skins, add to chili immediately, and stir. Add remaining ingredients and adjust for seasoning.

Sooner Gold

We are told that this recipe, or versions of it, has won lots of chili cook-offs in Oklahoma.

2   teaspoons cooking oil
3   pounds lean beef, cubed
2   13½-ounce cans beef broth
1   8-ounce can tomato sauce
Tabasco sauce to taste
2   teaspoons beef bouillon powder
1   teaspoon chicken bouillon powder
1½ teaspoons onion powder
1   teaspoon cayenne pepper
5-6 tablespoons chili powder
1-2 tablespoons cumin
1   teaspoon garlic powder
1   teaspoon white pepper

In a cooking pot, heat oil and cook meat until browned. Add broth, tomato sauce, Tabasco, beef and chicken bouillon powder, onion powder, and cayenne. Stir, bring to boil, cover, reduce heat, and let simmer for minimum of two hours. Add water as needed. Add chili powder, cumin, garlic powder, and white pepper, simmer for another thirty minutes, then serve.

Steak Chili

Not many chili recipes we've come across call for steak. This one was found in western Oklahoma and leads to a mighty delicious bowl of chili.

10   chiles, either Anaheim or ancho, dried, roasted, stemmed, peeled, and seeded

2½   cups beef or chicken broth

2   tablespoons olive oil

2-2½   pounds sirloin steak, cubed

Salt and pepper to taste

4   garlic cloves, minced

1   large onion, chopped

1   large and fresh jalapeño or serrano depending on taste, minced

1-2   tablespoons paprika

1   tablespoon chili powder

2   teaspoons cumin

1   28-ounce can tomatoes, crushed

2   tablespoons Worcestershire sauce

2   teaspoons oregano

2   teaspoons thyme

Blend dried chiles with one-half cup broth and allow to set for a few minutes. In a large cast-iron skillet, heat olive oil and brown the steak. Salt and pepper the meat as it cooks. Remove meat and set aside. Lower heat and add garlic, onion, and chile pepper and sauté. Add blended chiles, paprika, chili powder, and cumin and cook for another two to three minutes. Add remaining ingredients and allow to simmer for another one to one-and-a-half hours or until meat is tender. Adjust for seasonings. After ladling the chili into bowls, serve topped with cilantro.

Southwestern Chipotle Turkey Chili

This recipe puts leftover Thanksgiving turkey to good use. Wild turkey has been substituted on occasion with excellent results.

3	tablespoons olive oil
1	large onion, chopped
3	garlic cloves, minced
1	stalk celery, chopped
2	cups chicken broth
1½-2	pounds leftover turkey, chopped
3	chipotle chile peppers, stemmed, peeled, and chopped
1	8-ounce can tomato sauce
3	tablespoons chili powder
1	teaspoon cumin

Salt and pepper to taste

Heat oil in a cast-iron skillet and sauté onion, garlic, and celery. Place vegetables in a cooking pot, add turkey and broth, and bring to boil. Add chipotles, tomato sauce, chili powder, cumin, salt, and pepper. Stir, reduce heat, and allow to simmer for one hour. Add more broth if liquid is needed. Adjust for taste and serve with chopped fresh cilantro or parsley.

Taste of Texas Chili

As far as we can tell, this recipe, or a version of it, first appeared in a book entitled A Taste of Texas, edited by Jane Trahey and published in 1949. At the time, it was simply called a "Bowl of Red" and was submitted by a Mr. C.S. Boyles Jr. Since then, it has seen numerous reincarnations under various names, Taste of Texas Chili being our favorite.

2   tablespoons shortening
1   large onion, chopped
3   garlic cloves, minced
3   pounds lean beef, trimmed and coarse-ground
½   pound fresh unrendered suet
4   tablespoons chili powder
1   tablespoon cumin
1   tablespoon paprika
Salt and pepper to taste
2   quarts water

Heat shortening in cast-iron skillet and sauté onion and garlic. Add meat, chili powder, and cumin and continue to cook until meat is browned. Heat chopped suet in large cooking pot, add contents of skillet, stir, and cook for additional fifteen minutes. Add remaining ingredients, bring to boil, stir, reduce heat, and allow to simmer for at least two hours. Serve with crackers, tamales, or cheese.

In 1949 Mr. Boyles claimed the correct drink to accompany chili is either strong black coffee or an ice-cold beer.

Texas Beef and Pork Chili

The following is adapted from a championship recipe that includes pork as well as beef.

2 tablespoons olive oil
1 pound chuck, trimmed and cubed
2 teaspoons cumin
1 pound pork shoulder, trimmed and cubed
1 large onion, chopped
2 cloves garlic, minced
1 fresh tomato, chopped
3 stalks celery, chopped
1 8-ounce can green chili salsa
1 8-ounce can green chile peppers
1 teaspoon oregano
1 teaspoon Tabasco sauce
4 tablespoons chili powder
1 cup chicken broth
Salt and pepper to taste

In a cast-iron skillet heat oil, add beef and one-half teaspoon cumin, and brown meat. Remove, pat dry, set aside, add pork and remaining cumin, and brown meat. Remove, pat dry, and set aside. In a cooking pot, combine onion, garlic, tomato, celery, salsa, green chiles, oregano, Tabasco sauce, chili powder, broth, salt, and pepper. Stir, bring to boil, reduce heat, and simmer for one-half hour. Add meat to pot, stir, and simmer for additional one-and-a-half hours. Check for liquid, adding more broth if necessary. Adjust for seasoning. Serve topped with chopped fresh parsley.

Texas Red Chili

According to Joe Cooper, the first chili recipe ever recorded was credited to Barriga Aleana Corazon Contento. With very few changes, this basic recipe is still popular throughout Texas and the American Southwest today.

2 pounds beef, trimmed and cubed
8 dried red chile peppers, stemmed and seeded
2 garlic cloves, minced
1 teaspoon oregano
2 tablespoons flour
¼ cup cooking oil
1 teaspoon cumin
Salt to taste

Cover meat with water and boil for one-half hour, adding salt to taste. Save the water. At the same time the meat is cooking, soak dried chile peppers in water for one-half hour. Remove chiles and save this water, too. Mix the chiles with garlic and oregano and blend or grind to consistency of paste. Add one cup of water from the meat and one-half cup of water from the peppers. Heat cooking oil in a large cast-iron skillet and brown flour. Add the chile pepper paste and stir well. Add meat and, if necessary, additional beef water. Bring to boil, reduce heat, and allow to simmer for another hour. Serve with a side dish of pinto beans along with homemade corn tortillas.

Tequila Chili

Many chili cooks experiment from time to time by adding various kinds of alcoholic beverages to their concoctions. Tequila chili has been growing in popularity of late, and once you try a dish of this delectable preparation you will begin to understand why.

2	tablespoons olive oil
3	pounds beef shoulder, cubed
2	garlic cloves, minced
5	tablespoons mild ground red chile
1	tablespoon cumin
2	teaspoons cayenne
1	tablespoon oregano

Salt to taste

2	tablespoons chili powder
2	cups 100 percent blue agave tequila
5-6	cups water

Heat oil in large cast-iron chili pot, add meat, and brown. Stir in garlic, ground red chile, cumin, cayenne, oregano, salt, and chili powder, and let simmer for five minutes. Add tequila and water, bring to boil, reduce heat, and simmer for about two hours. Adjust seasonings for taste.

Trail Drive Chili

This recipe is believed to have had its origins in the 1880s.

10   dried ancho chiles, dried, roasted, peeled, stemmed, and seeded

4   chile pequins, dried and crushed

2   cups water

½-1 cup lard

5-6 garlic cloves, minced

4   large yellow onions, chopped

4   pounds beef chuck, cubed

2   tablespoons cumin

2   tablespoons oregano

Salt and pepper to taste

In a large cast-iron skillet, add anchos and chile pequins to water, bring to boil, then reduce heat and simmer for twenty minutes. Remove chiles and mince. Save water. In a cooking pot, heat lard, add garlic and onions, and sauté. Add meat and brown approximately ten minutes. Place chiles in pot along with cumin, oregano, salt, pepper, and about half of the saved water. Stir well, reduce heat, and allow to simmer for two hours, adding more water if necessary or, if you prefer, beer.

Turkey Chili

This is one of several innovative ways to put leftover Thanksgiving turkey to good use.

2   tablespoons olive oil
2   medium onions, chopped
1   stalk celery, chopped
1   fresh jalapeño chile pepper, minced
2   garlic cloves, minced
1   pound leftover turkey, chopped
2   16-ounce cans chicken broth
1   4½-ounce can chopped green chiles
1   cup corn
2   teaspoons cumin
2   teaspoons chili powder
Salt and black pepper to taste
½   cup chopped fresh cilantro

Heat olive oil in a large cooking pot, add onions, celery, jalapeño pepper, and garlic and sauté. Add turkey, broth, green chiles, corn, cumin, chili powder, salt, and pepper. Stir, bring to boil, reduce heat, and allow to simmer for twenty minutes. If beans are preferred, add one can of white beans. Serve with chopped fresh cilantro.

Turkey Chipotle Chili

The smoky flavor of chipotle, coupled with turkey, provides an incredibly delicious bowl of chili. Try serving this one to friends on a cold winter's eve. Chicken can be substituted for turkey in this recipe if you wish.

4   dried chipotle chile peppers
2   tablespoons olive oil
2   medium onions, chopped
3   garlic cloves, minced
3   pounds cooked, chopped turkey (leftover Thanksgiving turkey works fine!)
1   14½-ounce cans tomatoes
1-2 cups chicken broth
1   teaspoon cumin
1   teaspoon paprika
Salt and pepper to taste

Cut chipotle peppers in half, place in shallow bowl, and cover with boiling water. Set aside to rehydrate for thirty minutes. Heat olive oil in a cooking pot, add onions and garlic, and sauté. Place chipotles in a blender with a small amount of water and puree. Add turkey to pot, add puree, tomatoes (with liquid), broth, cumin, paprika, salt, and pepper. Stir, bring to boil, reduce heat, and let simmer for at least one hour. Add liquid if necessary and adjust for seasoning. Serve with chopped fresh cilantro.

Whiskey Chili

As with the aforementioned tequila chili, recipes calling for whiskey are also growing in popularity.

¼ cup bacon drippings
2-3 medium onions, chopped
3 cloves garlic, minced
3 pounds lean beef, cubed
2 16-ounce cans pinto beans
1 green bell pepper, chopped
2-3 cups whole tomatoes, peeled and seeded
1 16-ounce can tomato sauce
4 tablespoons chili powder
1 teaspoon basil
Salt, pepper, and paprika to taste
Tabasco to taste
½ cup jalapeño peppers, finely chopped
1 tablespoon brown sugar
2 cups whiskey

In a large cooking pot, heat bacon drippings, add onions and garlic, and sauté. Add meat and cook until browned. Add beans, bell pepper, tomatoes, tomato sauce, chili powder, basil, salt, pepper, paprika, Tabasco, jalapeños, and brown sugar. Stir well, reduce heat, cover, and simmer for one hour. Add whiskey, stir, and allow to simmer for another two hours or until meat is tender.

Whiskey Chili #2

6   dried Anaheim or ancho chiles, stemmed and seeded

1   bottle dark Mexican beer

2   tablespoons olive oil

2   medium onions, chopped

3   garlic cloves, minced

1   fresh jalapeño, stemmed, seeded, and chopped

2   pounds lean beef, trimmed and cubed

1   8-ounce can tomato sauce

½   cup whiskey

2   teaspoons cumin

1   teaspoon paprika

1   teaspoon oregano

Salt and pepper to taste

Cut dried chiles in half, place in shallow bowl, and cover with beer for one hour. Stir from time to time to make certain all chiles are exposed to the liquid. Heat olive oil in a cast-iron skillet; add onions, garlic, and jalapeño and sauté. Add meat and cook until browned. Place meat and vegetables in a cooking pot, add tomato sauce, whiskey, cumin, paprika, oregano, salt, and pepper. Stir, bring to boil, reduce heat, and simmer for two hours. As chili begins to simmer, place reconstituted chiles in a blender, puree to a paste, remove skins, and add to chili. Adjust for seasonings and whiskey.

Whiskey Chili #3

I *first sampled this recipe during a cool autumn evening while sitting out on the back porch. Along with the sound of the birds calling in the trees and smells of the season wafting through the air, this chili hit the spot and added to the magic of that day.*

2   tablespoons olive oil
2-2½   pounds coarsely ground beef
1   cup beef broth
1   8-ounce can tomato sauce
1½   tablespoons onion powder
1   tablespoon garlic powder
1   teaspoon beef bouillon crystals
3   teaspoons cumin
2   teaspoons crushed red pepper
Salt to taste
5   tablespoons chili powder
2   teaspoons paprika
1   cup whiskey

In a large cooking pot, heat oil and brown beef. Add broth, tomato sauce, one tablespoon onion powder, garlic powder, and bouillon crystals. Add enough water to cover, stir, bring to boil, reduce heat, and let simmer for one hour. Add two teaspoons cumin, one teaspoon red pepper, salt, the remaining onion powder, and four tablespoons chili powder, stir, and allow to simmer for another hour. Add water if necessary. Add remaining red pepper, paprika, remaining chili powder, and whiskey. Stir, and cook for another thirty minutes.

Yankee Chili

This recipe was sent to me by a friend who lives in Maine, close to the farthest extent of Yankeedom. Though he as well as the people he prepares chili for are partial to kidney beans and hamburger, this recipe also employs a number of traditional ingredients and yields a pretty fair bowl of chili.

2	pounds ground beef
3	tablespoons olive oil
1	large onion chopped
3	garlic cloves, minced
1	red bell pepper, chopped

Salt and pepper to taste

1	teaspoon cumin
½	teaspoon ground chipotle pepper
1	teaspoon crushed red pepper
3	tablespoons chili powder
2	cups beef broth
1	26-ounce can crushed tomatoes
2	16-ounce cans kidney beans, drained

Place ground beef in a large cooking pot and brown. Drain and set aside. Add olive oil, heat, and sauté onion, garlic, and red bell pepper. Add salt, pepper, cumin, chipotle, crushed red pepper, and chili powder, and stir. Add broth and tomatoes, stir, bring to boil, reduce heat, and allow to simmer for about two hours. Add beans and simmer for an additional thirty minutes. Serve with fresh chopped parsley and sourdough bread.

Wild Game Chili

A variety of wild game seems made to order for chili. Since, as we stated in an earlier chapter, meat is the heart of chili, it stands to reason that a number of different kinds of meat could be employed in the making of a good pot of chili.

Beef, of course, appears to be meat of choice among a large number of chili cooks, but a number of outdoorsmen and sportsmen have successfully incorporated venison, elk, buffalo, wild turkey, rabbit, and even rattlesnake into their chili recipes.

The results are uncommonly delicious, the recipes are generally easy to follow, and the use to which the wild game is put in the making of chili simply adds another dimension to the hunt as well as to the kitchen.

Buffalo Chili

Buffalo is becoming a preferred meat among many who like the lower fat and cholesterol content. In addition, it is simply delicious.

3	tablespoons olive oil
3	pounds buffalo meat, cubed
1	large Vidalia onion, chopped
3	garlic cloves, minced
2	cups chicken broth
2	8-ounce cans tomato sauce
6	tablespoons chili powder
2	tablespoons cumin
1	tablespoon oregano

Salt and pepper to taste

1   teaspoon Tabasco sauce

Heat oil in a large cast-iron skillet and brown buffalo meat. Remove meat to large cooking pot. Sauté onion and garlic in the skillet, place in pot, add broth, stir, and simmer for one hour. Add tomato sauce, chili powder, cumin, oregano, salt, and pepper. Stir and continue to simmer for additional one-half hour. Fifteen minutes prior to serving, add Tabasco sauce.

Elk Chili

Each year hundreds of chili-loving Texans travel to Colorado and Wyoming to hunt elk and deer. Combining the meat from their harvest with their cultural need for a good bowl of chili, a number of recipes evolved. The one below has undergone several modifications and experiments in my own kitchen until I finally arrived at what I consider the perfect palate-pleasing concoction. This recipe is as easy to prepare in hunting camp as it is in the kitchen.

2	pounds elk meat, coarsely ground or finely chopped
2-3	cups water
1	large onion, chopped
2	garlic cloves, minced
1	8-ounce can tomato sauce
4	tablespoons chili powder
1	teaspoon cumin
1	teaspoon oregano
1	teaspoon paprika
3	teaspoons Worcestershire sauce
5	whole cloves

Salt and pepper to taste

In a large cooking pot, add elk and water, bring to boil, and cook until meat is tender. Add onion, garlic, tomato sauce, chili powder, cumin, oregano, paprika, Worcestershire sauce, cloves, salt, and pepper. Stir, reduce heat slightly, and cook for another one-half hour. Check for liquid and seasoning, reduce heat to simmer, and cook for an additional two hours.

Elk Chili #2

Try this variation on the previous elk chili recipe.

3 tablespoons olive oil
1 large onion, chopped
4 garlic cloves, minced
1½ pounds elk meat, chopped
1 teaspoon cayenne
1 teaspoon cumin
1 teaspoon crushed red pepper
1 teaspoon oregano
Salt and pepper to taste
2 15-ounce cans tomatoes
1 16-ounce can pinto beans
1-2 fresh jalapeño chile peppers, chopped

Heat olive oil in large cast-iron skillet and sauté onion and garlic. Add meat and cook until brown. Add cayenne, cumin, crushed red pepper, oregano, salt, and pepper. Stir, reduce heat slightly, and cook for ten minutes. Add canned beans and tomatoes, including the liquid, stir, bring to boil for ten minutes, reduce heat, and simmer for one-and-a-half to two hours. Add chopped jalapeño chiles approximately one-half hour before serving.

Javelina Chili

T*he javelina, as most Southwesterners know, is a pig-like animal that frequents the desert areas along the Mexican border. Many years ago, javelina hunters discovered the flesh from this creature yields a delicious taste that provides for a fine pot of chili.*

3   pounds javelina shoulder, cubed
2   tablespoons cooking oil
Salt to taste
2   garlic cloves, minced
4-6 tablespoons chili powder
½   teaspoon Mexican oregano
3   cups pork or chicken broth
2-4 cups cooked pinto beans, depending on taste
     (optional)

Using a cast-iron skillet, brown the meat over a medium-high heat. (If you are not overly cholesterol conscious, the fat from the butchered javelina can be used instead of cooking oil.) Add salt and garlic, mix well, and reduce heat. Add chili powder and oregano, stirring well to make certain meat is coated. This done, add broth to a depth of one-quarter inch. Stir and simmer for an hour, adding broth as needed. When the appropriate time has elapsed, taste and adjust seasonings. Cook until meat is very tender, and serve, offering the pinto beans as a side dish.

Javelina Chili #2

The secret behind this robust wild game chili is the use of smoked paprika.

2   tablespoons olive oil
2   pounds javelina meat, trimmed and cubed
2   onions, chopped
3   garlic cloves, minced
1   stalk celery, chopped
3   cans chicken broth
1   8-ounce can tomato sauce
2   tablespoons smoked paprika
2   tablespoons chili powder
1   teaspoon oregano
Salt and pepper to taste

Heat olive oil in a large cooking pot, add meat, and brown. Add onions, garlic, and celery, and sauté. Add broth, tomato sauce, paprika, chili powder, oregano, salt, and pepper. Stir, bring to boil, reduce heat, and let simmer for two hours stirring often. Serve with wild rice.

Rabbit Chili
(Chili de Conejo)

I *was once told that during the times when it was hard for poor families to acquire beef, they often had to rely on the bounty of the land to provide what foods they consumed. Wild game, including rabbits, often served as an acceptable alternative. It was only a small step to begin substituting rabbit for beef in chili, and the result proved to be well worth the experiment.*

3 tablespoons olive oil
1 onion, chopped
2 garlic cloves, minced
¼ cup pine nuts
2 cups chicken broth
1 large tomato, peeled and chopped
2 tomatillos, peeled and chopped
2 fresh jalapeño or serrano chile peppers, chopped
2 pounds rabbit meat, trimmed
Salt and pepper to taste

In a large cast-iron skillet, heat oil, add onion, garlic, and pine nuts, and sauté. Add chicken broth, tomato, tomatillos, and chile peppers. Stir and cook for additional twenty to thirty minutes. As this is cooking, rub some olive oil onto rabbit, add salt and pepper, and grill over medium heat for ten minutes, turning often. When done, cut into one-half-inch thick slices or cubes. Pour chili into bowls, top with rabbit meat, garnish with parsley, and serve.

Rattlesnake Chili

It is likely that the first time rattlesnake meat was used to make chili it was done so out of necessity or perhaps as a novelty. The truth is, rattlesnake chili, in addition to being unusual, is good and tasty.

6	dried ancho chiles
2	pounds boned rattlesnake meat
1½	pounds link sausage, diced
1	large onion, chopped
3	garlic cloves, minced
4	4-ounce cans chopped green chiles
4	large tomatoes
2	teaspoons cumin
2	teaspoons paprika
1	teaspoon Mexican oregano

Remove stems and seeds from anchos, place in pot of boiling water, and simmer for approximately one hour. Remove from water, peel away skins, and blend until pureed. Brown rattlesnake meat, sausage, onion, and garlic in cast-iron skillet. Add green chiles, tomatoes, and spices while stirring. Add half of the ancho puree, mix well, and allow to simmer for about two hours. As liquid is needed, add beer or water. After one hour add more ancho puree if needed.

Uncle Charley's Rattlesnake Chili

Uncle Charley was a crusty old West Texas ranch foreman who could make chili out of anything. Those fortunate enough to have known him were often invited to dine on chili made from antelope, prairie dog, crow, and raccoon. His specialty, however, was rattlesnake chili. During the summer, Uncle Charley would drive his 1949 Chevrolet pickup around the ranch in search of rattlesnakes just to use in chili.

2 tablespoons olive oil
3 pounds lean sirloin, cubed
1 pound pork sausage
3 garlic gloves, minced
3 medium onions, chopped
2 green bell peppers, chopped
1 pound rattlesnake meat
3 cans stewed tomatoes
3 cans tomato sauce
1 bottle Mexican beer
2 tablespoons brown sugar
¼ cup Worcestershire sauce
6 tablespoons chili powder
1 tablespoon oregano
2 teaspoons cumin
Salt and cayenne pepper to taste
1-2 15-ounce cans pinto beans
1 can garbanzos
1-2 cups cooked white rice

In a large cast-iron skillet, heat oil, add beef, sausage, garlic, onions, and bell peppers and cook until meat is browned. Drain, and place in cooking pot. After making certain the rattlesnake meat is boned, add it to the pot along with tomatoes, tomato sauce, beer, brown sugar, and Worcestershire sauce. Bring to boil, then lower heat and add chili powder, oregano, cumin, salt, and cayenne pepper. Stir well and simmer for at least one hour. Add pinto beans and garbanzos after draining water from the cans and cook for another hour, adding more beer or water if necessary. Serve over rice.

Venison Chili #1

The old gentleman who gave me this recipe for venison chili many years ago explained that he sometimes adds all or some of the following ingredients: brown sugar, lemon, mustard, and vinegar. These are items not normally found in chili but, he claims, actually help in removing the sometimes strong gamey taste of the deer while enhancing the flavor.

1 tablespoon olive oil
2 pounds deer roast, cubed
1-2 onions, chopped
1-2 cloves garlic, minced
2 cans tomatoes, chopped
3-4 tablespoons chili powder
1 tablespoon oregano
½ tablespoon cumin
1 teaspoon paprika
Salt and pepper to taste

In a large cast-iron skillet, heat oil, add deer meat, and brown. (Some positive results have occurred as a result of marinating the meat overnight in a mixture of red wine, soy sauce, and vinegar.) Add onions and garlic and sauté for an additional four to five minutes. Add the remaining ingredients, stir well, bring to boil, reduce heat, and simmer. If more liquid is desired, add water or beer. Serve with wild rice and steamed carrots.

Venison Chili #2

This venison chili recipe is somewhat unique in that it contains mushrooms. 'Shrooms are rarely added to chili and for a lot of good reasons. In this case, however, they have a positive effect, yielding a flavorful dish that fairly explodes with exciting taste!

1	ounce dried mushrooms, shitakes preferred
½	cup bourbon, seven-year-old Jim Beam recommended
2	tablespoons olive oil
2	garlic cloves, minced
2	shallots, minced
1-2	fresh jalapeño chiles
2	pounds coarsely ground venison
4	tablespoons chili powder
1	tablespoon ground cumin
1	teaspoon oregano
1	teaspoon thyme
3-4	cups Mexican beer, preferably Dos Equis
1	14½-ounce can crushed tomatoes

Salt and pepper to taste

2	tablespoons masa harina, if desired

Marinate dried mushrooms in bourbon overnight. In a large cast-iron skillet, heat olive oil, add garlic, shallots, and jalapeños, and sauté. Add venison and cook until meat is well browned. Stir in chili powder, cumin, oregano, and thyme, and cook for another two minutes. Drain mushrooms and add to skillet, stirring well. Add as much of the bourbon marinade as you wish, along with beer, tomatoes, salt, and pepper. Bring to boil, reduce heat, and allow to simmer for at least one hour. If a thicker chili is desired, make a paste with masa harina and water and add it. If a thinner chili is more to your taste, add water or bourbon. Garnish with chopped fresh cilantro and serve with freshly baked sourdough bread.

Venison Chili #3
(Texas Deer Camp Chili)

Easy to prepare yet incredibly tasty, my first encounter with this version of venison chili was in a Southwest Texas deer camp.

4	tablespoons olive oil
2	onions, chopped
5	garlic cloves, minced
3	ancho chile peppers, stemmed, seeded, and chopped
2	pounds venison, cubed
1	tablespoon coarse-ground red pepper
4	tomatoes, chopped
1	teaspoon cumin
2	cans beef or chicken broth

Salt and black pepper to taste

In a large cast-iron skillet, heat olive oil, add onions, garlic, and chile peppers, and sauté. Add venison and cook until meat has browned. Add red pepper, tomatoes, cumin, and broth. Stir and simmer for two hours. During the simmering time, stir the mix and adjust for taste. When I make this for company, I serve it with cheese and jalapeño quesadillas.

Venison Chili #4
(Brewster County Deer Chili)

*S*ome mighty fine wild game chile recipes have come out of Brewster County, Texas. This is one that has stood the test over the years.

3   pounds venison, trimmed and cubed
4-5 tablespoons flour
3   tablespoons chili powder
3   tablespoons cooking oil
2   large onions, chopped
2   garlic cloves, minced
2   cups tomato sauce
2   fresh tomatoes, seeded, skinned, and pulped
2   dozen ground dried chile pequins (If unavailable, use 4 dried ground Anaheim chile peppers.)
1   teaspoon oregano
1   teaspoon cumin
1   teaspoon paprika
Salt to taste

In a large bowl, add venison, flour, and chili powder and mix until meat is coated. Heat oil in a large cooking pot and sauté onions and garlic. Add meat and brown. Add tomato sauce, tomatoes, chiles, oregano, cumin, paprika, and salt. Stir well and add enough water to cover. Simmer for three to four hours, stirring occasionally and adding water as needed and adjusting for seasonings. Serve with wild rice or roasted potatoes.

Venison Chili #5
(Hudspeth County Deer and Cactus Chili)

The nopalitos called for in this recipe are pickled prickly pear cactus pads, a long-overlooked culinary resource very few people have taken advantage of.

3	tablespoons olive oil
1	large onion, chopped
3	garlic cloves, minced
2	pounds venison, cubed
1	bottle dark Mexican beer
1	8-ounce can tomato sauce
4	tablespoons chili powder
1	teaspoon cumin
1	teaspoon oregano
1	teaspoon thyme
1	teaspoon cayenne

Salt and pepper to taste

1	11-ounce jar nopalitos
1	15-ounce can pinto beans (optional)

In a large cast-iron skillet, heat oil and sauté onion and garlic, add venison, and continue cooking until meat is browned. Add beer and tomato sauce, stir, bring to boil, reduce heat, and simmer for at least one hour. As mixture begins to simmer, add chili powder, cumin, oregano, thyme, cayenne, salt, and pepper. Fifteen minutes before serving, drain the nopalitos (and the beans, if using them) and stir into mixture. Serve with chopped fresh parsley.

Wild Duck Chili

There are a number of ways to prepare wild duck, but few avid duck hunters are aware of its use in chili. Contrary to what many chili purists may believe, duck chili is a delicious feast, one that will quickly rise to the top of your list of favorites.

2 tablespoons olive oil
2 onions, chopped
2 garlic cloves, minced
2 duck breasts, skinned, boned, and chopped
2 tablespoons chili powder
2 tablespoons Mexican paprika
1 tablespoon cumin
1 14½-ounce can crushed tomatoes
1 cup chicken broth
½ cup fresh cilantro, chopped
1 tablespoon oregano
Salt and white pepper to taste

In a large cast-iron skillet, heat oil and sauté onions and garlic. Add wild duck and cook until browned, approximately five to ten minutes. Add chili powder, paprika, and cumin; stir and cook for another five minutes. Add tomatoes, chicken broth, cilantro, oregano, salt, and pepper. Bring to boil, reduce heat, then simmer for one-half to one hour. Try serving this unique chili over steamed rice for a truly different wild game treat.

Wild Duck Chili #2
(Duck and Mushroom Chili)

A chili-cooking friend who loves to experiment with wild game recipes insists that few cultures know how to prepare duck as well as the Chinese, a culture which has long teamed particular spices and herbs with this meat. Hence, he claims, a wild duck chili should list among its ingredients such traditionally Oriental blending of ginger, peanut oil, and soy sauce.

1 cup dried mushrooms, preferably shitake
2 tablespoons peanut oil
2 garlic cloves, minced
2 shallots, chopped
2 fresh serrano chile peppers, stemmed, seeded, and minced
1 teaspoon ginger root, minced
2 pounds wild duck breasts, skinned, boned, and chopped
1 tablespoon chili powder
1 tablespoon cumin seeds
1 tablespoon Mexican paprika
2 cups beer
1 can chicken broth
1 14½-ounce can crushed tomatoes
2 tablespoons soy sauce
2 tablespoons fresh cilantro, chopped
Salt and pepper to taste

Soak mushrooms in hot water for no more than thirty minutes. Drain, remove and discard stems, slice caps 1/4 inch wide, and set aside. In a large cooking pot or skillet, heat oil; add garlic, shallots, serrano chiles, and ginger root, and sauté. Add wild duck and brown for approximately seven to eight minutes. Add chili powder, cumin seeds, and paprika; mix well and cook for another two minutes. Add beer, chicken broth, tomatoes, soy sauce, cilantro, salt, and pepper. Bring to boil, reduce heat, and allow to simmer for one-half hour. Taste and adjust for seasoning. Serve over rice.

Wild Turkey Chili

*O*ne of the best uses to which one can put wild turkey is in chili. The following recipe comes from an Oklahoma chilisto who would rather have his game turkey in a pot o' red than any other way.

4-6	slices bacon
1	tablespoon olive oil
3	large yellow onions, chopped
1	tablespoon fresh cilantro, chopped
1	tablespoon tarragon
1	chipotle or ancho chile, peeled, seeded, and chopped
1-2	bay leaves
2	teaspoons cumin
¼	cup red wine
5-6	cups chicken stock
4	4-ounce cans chopped green chiles
2	cans pinto beans, drained
2	teaspoon Worcestershire sauce

Salt and pepper to taste

2-3   pounds wild turkey, smoked and cubed

In a large cast-iron skillet, cook bacon until not quite crisp, drain, cut into small pieces, and return to pan. Add oil and sauté onions, cilantro, tarragon, chile, bay leaves, and cumin. After five to ten minutes, drain, add wine, stir, and cook additional five minutes. Add remaining ingredients and simmer for thirty to forty-five minutes.

Wild Turkey Chili #2

As with the previous recipe, this one comes from the great state of Oklahoma.

1-2　tablespoons olive oil

1-2　pounds wild turkey, coarsely ground

2-3　large yellow onions, chopped

2　garlic cloves, minced

1　28-ounce can crushed tomatoes

1　10-ounce can diced tomatoes with green chiles

2-3　cups water

Salt and pepper to taste

½　teaspoon oregano

1　tablespoon cumin

1　tablespoon Worcestershire sauce

2　tablespoons chili powder

2　cans pinto beans, drained

In large cast-iron skillet, heat oil, add turkey, and brown. Add onions and garlic and sauté until onions are translucent. Add crushed tomatoes, diced tomatoes with green chiles, water to cover, salt, pepper, oregano, cumin, Worcestershire, and chili powder. Bring to boil, lower heat, and simmer for one hour. Add pinto beans, cook for additional fifteen to thirty minutes, and serve.

Wild Turkey Chili #3
(Minnesota Wild Turkey Chili)

While this recipe comes from a Minnesota friend, it contains some traditional Southwestern ingredients, most notably tomatillos. Added to this delightful pot of chili are Great Northern beans, which somehow provide an additional dimension and a totally acceptable taste.

2 tablespoons cooking oil

4 fresh Anaheim chiles, peeled, stemmed, and chopped

2 garlic cloves, minced

1 onion, chopped

2 pounds coarsely ground or finely chopped wild turkey

4 cups chicken broth

2 cups fresh tomatillos, chopped

1 teaspoon oregano

1 teaspoon cumin

1 teaspoon thyme

Salt and pepper to taste

2 cups cooked Great Northern beans

In a large cast-iron skillet, heat oil, add Anaheim chiles, garlic, and onion, and sauté. Add turkey, mix well, and cook until browned. Add chicken broth, tomatillos, oregano, cumin, thyme, salt, pepper, and beans, stir, and bring to boil. Reduce heat and simmer for one hour, adjusting for taste and liquid. If more liquid is needed, add chicken broth or beer. Garnish with chopped fresh cilantro or green onion and serve with fresh bread.

Wild Turkey Chili #4
(Chihuahuan Tequila and Turkey Chili)

This recipe returned with us from a successful turkey-hunting trip deep into the Sierra Madres in the Mexican state of Chihuahua. Although the natives who prepared it for us referred to it as a stew, it has all the earmarks of a wonderful wild turkey chili.

2   tablespoons cooking oil
4   garlic cloves, minced
2-3 onions, chopped
2-3 tablespoons chili powder
1   tablespoon cumin seeds
1   teaspoon crushed red pepper
2   tablespoons fresh chopped cilantro
2   pounds ground wild turkey
1   28-ounce can crushed tomatoes
½   cup 100 percent blue agave tequila
¼   cup fresh-squeezed lime juice
1   tablespoon oregano
2   teaspoons basil
Salt to taste
White pepper to taste

In a large cooking pot, heat oil and sauté garlic, onions, chili powder, cumin seeds, red pepper, and cilantro all together. Add ground wild turkey, stir, raise heat slightly, and brown the meat for approximately ten minutes. Add tomatoes, tequila, lime juice, oregano, basil, salt, and white pepper. Stir well, bring to boil, reduce heat, and allow to simmer for one to one-and-a-half hours. If more liquid is needed, add tequila. If a thicker chili is desired, mix a paste of masa harina and water and add as much as needed.

Note: If 100 percent blue agave tequila is unavailable, 51 percent tequila such as Jose Cuervo Gold may be used, although some of the high-quality tequila taste is sacrificed. Likewise, bottled lime juice may be used, but fresh lime juice is preferable.

Wild Turkey Chili #5

This wild turkey recipe has a distinctive French attitude with red wine and mushrooms among the ingredients. Like the previous recipe, this one also comes from Mexico.

2	tablespoons olive oil
3	onions, chopped
3	garlic cloves, minced
1	tablespoon paprika, Hungarian preferred
1	teaspoon crushed red pepper
1	teaspoon cumin
1	teaspoon cilantro
1½	pounds ground wild turkey
2	cups mushrooms, chopped
1	28-ounce can crushed tomatoes
1	cup dry red wine
1	tablespoon oregano
2	teaspoons dried leaf basil
½	teaspoon thyme

Salt and pepper to taste

In a large cooking pot, heat oil and sauté onions, garlic, paprika, red pepper, cumin, and cilantro. Add turkey, stir, and increase heat. Cook long enough to brown the meat. Add mushrooms, tomatoes, red wine, oregano, basil, thyme, salt, and pepper. Bring to boil, reduce heat, and let simmer for one to one-and-a-half hours. Stir occasionally and adjust for taste. If thicker chili is desired, add a paste made from masa harina and water. If a thinner chile is desired, try adding chicken broth.

Wild Turkey Chili #6
(Mountain Man Turkey Chili)

This recipe was adapted from one given to me by an avid wild turkey hunter who prepared this dish in camp, always to the rousing cheers of his companions. This recipe was also once followed using leftover Thanksgiving turkey with excellent results.

4	dried Anaheim chile peppers, stemmed, seeded, peeled, and chopped
4	tablespoons olive oil
2	pounds finely chopped wild turkey meat
2	cups chicken broth
1	large onion, chopped
2	garlic cloves, minced
1	stalk celery, chopped
2	fresh jalapeño chile peppers
1	15-ounce can crushed tomatoes
½	teaspoon sage
1	teaspoon oregano
Salt and peppers to taste	
1	15-ounce can kidney beans

Place dried Anaheims in a bowl and cover with boiling water, stir, and set aside for thirty minutes. Heat two tablespoons olive oil in cast-iron skillet, add turkey, and brown. Drain, pat meat dry with paper towel and place into cooking pot. Add chicken broth, bring to boil, reduce heat, and simmer. Wipe residue from skillet with a paper towel, then heat remaining olive oil, add onion, garlic, and celery, sauté, and add to pot along with jalapeño peppers, tomatoes (including liquid), sage, oregano, salt, and pepper, and stir. Bring to boil, reduce heat, and simmer for one hour. As the simmering process begins, mash the reconstituted chile peppers, add to pot, and stir. Fifteen minutes before serving, add kidney beans. Adjust for seasoning.

Seafood Chili

*T*o many who claim to be dyed-in-the-wool chili cooks and diners, the notion of making this special dish out of seafood may likely be met with sneers and jeers.

While the nation's fraternity of serious and professional chilistos tends to be a rather conservative lot, a growing number, who possess a distinct sense of adventure and a zest for trying something new, find a lot of good things about seafood chili and, in fact, are preparing it more and more.

The following recipes show you some delicious and exciting things that can be done with bass, scallops, shrimp, and crabmeat. Don't knock seafood chili until you've tried it. Once you do, I'm convinced you will be a believer like hundreds of others.

Bass Grill Chili

This is another recipe adapted from a Mexican dish. In this case, it was found in a quiet little restaurant near the shores of Lake Boquillas located not far from Ciudad Camargo in the state of Chihuahua. They do some magic things with bass and chile peppers down there, and this is one of them.

3 tablespoons cooking oil
2 tablespoons chili powder
1 teaspoon Mexican paprika
2 pounds black bass filets
1 cup fish broth
1-2 cups cooked pinto beans
1 cup green chiles, chopped
Salt and white pepper to taste

In a bowl, mix oil, chili powder, and paprika. Dredge bass filets through this mixture, assuring each piece is well coated. Grill seven to eight minutes on each side over medium heat. In a cooking vessel, combine broth, pinto beans, green chiles, salt, and pepper, stir well, and cook for several minutes. Spoon the mix into a shallow bowl or plate, place grilled bass on top, garnish with fresh chopped cilantro, and serve.

Catfish Chili

While mostly a lake and river denizen, catfish will be included in this section merely out of convenience.

10	dried ancho or Anaheim chiles, stemmed, seeded, and roasted
2	cups fish broth
3	tablespoons olive oil
4	medium shallots, chopped
2	garlic cloves, minced
1	teaspoon cumin
4	tomatoes, chopped
2	teaspoons oregano
1	teaspoon basil

Salt and pepper to taste

2	tablespoons chili powder
1	teaspoon coriander
2	pounds catfish filets

Placed dried chiles in a blender along with one cup of fish broth and process until pureed. In a large skillet, heat oil, add shallots and garlic, and sauté. Stir in cumin, cook for another five to ten minutes, then add pureed chiles. Mix well and cook for two more minutes. Add remaining fish broth, tomatoes, oregano, basil, salt, and pepper. Bring to boil, reduce heat, and allow to simmer for one-half hour or until sauce has thickened. In a bowl, mix chili powder, coriander, salt, and pepper. Rub this mixture into the catfish filets and grill for approximately five minutes per side. When fish is done, cut into slices and add to the mix. Allow to cook for another ten minutes, then serve over rice and garnish with rosemary, chives, or chopped fresh cilantro.

Crabmeat Chili

*F*resh crabmeat is best if you can get it, but a few recent experiments with canned crab meat have proven quite satisfactory.

6 tablespoons unsalted butter
4 tablespoons olive oil
1 shallot, chopped
1 garlic clove, minced
2 teaspoons dried red chile, crushed
1 teaspoon paprika
1 pound crabmeat, shredded
Salt and white pepper to taste

In a cooking pot, heat unsalted butter and olive oil, add shallot and garlic, and sauté. Add crushed red chile and paprika, stir, and cook for another two minutes. Add crabmeat, salt, and pepper, mix well, and continue to cook for ten more minutes. Serve over rice and garnish with fresh chopped cilantro.

Carlos' Lobster Chili

As a result of a dare, I arrived at the following recipe, which includes lobster and black beans.

3   tablespoons olive oil
4   shallots, chopped
2   garlic cloves, minced
10 fresh ancho chile peppers
1   cup cooked black beans
2   cups fish broth
1   14½-ounce can crushed tomatoes
1   tablespoon oregano
½   tablespoon basil
1   teaspoon thyme
Salt and pepper to taste
½   stick butter, melted
4   lobster tails
2   tablespoons Hungarian paprika

In a cast-iron skillet, heat oil, add shallots, garlic, and chile peppers, and sauté. Place in cooking pot and add beans, fish broth, tomatoes, oregano, basil, thyme, salt, and pepper. Bring to boil, reduce heat, and simmer for one-half hour. In a separate saucepan, boil water and blanch lobster tails, drain, shell, and pat dry. Cut tails into three-quarter-inch slices, place in shallow dish, add melted butter and make certain the pieces of lobster are well coated. Season with paprika and grill for one minute each side. Serve the chili mix in bowls, top with lobster, and garnish with fresh cilantro or parsley.

Scallop Chili

Scallops are a tiny yet tasty marine bivalve, and they provide the essential flavor and texture for this exciting dish.

4	tablespoons unsalted butter
3	tablespoons olive oil
1	shallot, chopped
2	garlic cloves, minced
4	fresh Anaheims, peeled, seeded, stemmed, and chopped
2	green or red bell peppers, chopped
2	pounds scallops
1	fresh lime

Salt and pepper to taste

In a large cast-iron skillet, heat butter and oil, add shallot, garlic, chile peppers, and bell peppers, and sauté. Add scallops and cook over medium heat for another five minutes. Squeeze juice from the lime into the skillet, salt and pepper to taste, and serve with steamed rice.

Shrimp Chili

Unlike chili made from beef and other red meats, shrimp chili doesn't need much simmering time and can be ready to eat only minutes after beginning preparation.

4	tablespoons cooking oil
2	medium onions, chopped
4	garlic cloves, minced
4	Anaheim chile peppers, stemmed, seeded, and diced
1	pound fresh shrimp, shelled
¼	cup fresh cilantro, chopped
¼	cup fresh parsley, chopped

Salt and white pepper to taste

In a large cast-iron skillet, heat oil, add onions, garlic, and chiles, and sauté. Add shrimp, stir, and cook another two to three minutes. Add cilantro, parsley, salt, and white pepper, stir, and cook for an additional two minutes. Delicious served over rice.

Cajun Shrimp Chili

In the opinion of many, some of the country's finest cooks are found in southern Louisiana. The following recipe is the result of numerous trips to Cajun country and exploring the various ways in which they prepare shrimp.

4	tablespoons olive oil
1	onion, chopped
2	garlic cloves, minced
6	fresh chiles, either Anaheim, ancho, or jalapeño, depending on preference
2	cups cooked Great Northern beans
4	cups fish broth
2	cups tomatillos, chopped
1	tablespoon oregano
1	teaspoon dried leaf basil
1	teaspoon thyme

Salt and white pepper to taste

2	tablespoons chili powder
1	tablespoon Mexican paprika
1½-2	pounds fresh shrimp, shelled

In a cooking pot, heat olive oil and sauté onion, garlic, and chile peppers. Add beans, broth, tomatillos, oregano, basil, thyme, salt, and white pepper. Stir, bring to boil, then reduce heat and let simmer for one-half hour. If necessary, add liquid (water or beer). Add chili powder and paprika, stir, and simmer another fifteen minutes. Rub shrimp with butter, season with paprika, and sauté in slightly buttered pan until blackened. Add to chili mixture, stir, and serve with a fresh chopped cilantro garnish.

Health Food and Vegetarian Chili

*I*n order to derive a pot of high-quality chili with little or no meat, one that could hold its own with those who are fanatic about taste, bold approaches to altering and adding certain ingredients were called for. A lot of work and experimentation went into testing quantities and kinds of chile peppers as well as other ingredients. Experiments of this nature are continuing, but we remain happy with our results thus far, many of which are presented in the following pages.

Bean Chili a la Birmingham

While the pinto bean is the legume of choice in Texas and the American Southwest, the black-eyed pea dominates in much of the South. It is no surprise, then, to discover chili made with them. The following recipe, as far as we can discern, had its origins in Birmingham, Alabama, but was experimented with and refined in various Texas kitchens until we arrived at one we could serve proudly to health-conscious friends. The Birmingham version called for sugar and vinegar, neither of which actually adds much to a serious chili recipe. If your tastes run in that direction, however, feel free to add them.

3   pounds fresh black-eyed peas
3   tablespoons olive oil
2   onions, chopped
2   garlic cloves, minced
4   fresh Anaheim chile peppers, stemmed, seeded, and chopped
2   fresh jalapeño chile peppers, stemmed, seeded, and chopped
1   pound fresh tomatoes, chopped
¼   cup fresh cilantro, chopped
2   tablespoons oregano
Salt and pepper to taste

In a cooking pot, add black-eyed peas to boiling water and cook for two to three minutes. Drain, rinse, and set aside while you prepare other ingredients. In a cast-iron skillet heat olive oil, add onions, garlic, and chile peppers, and sauté. Add black-eyed peas, tomatoes, cilantro, oregano, salt, and pepper, and cook for another ten to fifteen minutes or until peas are tender. This yields a relatively thick chili. If a thinner one is desired, add some tomato juice. In Birmingham, they served this over rice and garnished it with fresh chopped parsley or cilantro.

Bean Chili a la Chicago

In those parts of the country where one finds significant populations of vegetarians, one can also find some innovative recipes for a variety of meatless chile dishes. The following recipe was encountered in a health food restaurant in suburban Chicago.

1   pound dried Great Northern beans
2   tablespoons olive oil
2   onions, chopped
3   garlic cloves, minced
4   fresh Anaheim chile peppers
2   fresh jalapeño chile peppers
1   tablespoon cumin
1   teaspoon crushed red pepper
6   cups chicken broth
2   cups sun-dried tomatoes, chopped
2   tablespoons oregano
1   cup parsley
Salt and pepper to taste

In a cooking pot, cover Great Northern beans with water and bring to boil for five minutes. Remove pot and set aside, allowing beans to soak for one hour. While beans are soaking, heat olive oil, add onions, garlic, and chile peppers, and sauté. Add cumin and red pepper, stir, and cook for another minute. Add beans (including the water) and chicken broth, stir well, and bring to boil. While you are waiting for the mix to boil, stir in one cup of sun-dried tomatoes, oregano, parsley, salt, and pepper. Reduce heat and let simmer for two hours or until beans are tender. At that point, add the last cup of sun-dried tomatoes, cook for another fifteen minutes, and serve.

When we first dined on Bean Chili *a la* Chicago, it was accompanied by homemade wheat crackers, a side we have enjoyed duplicating each time we prepare this dish.

Bean Chili a la Thibodeaux

This vegetarian chili dish was discovered one early morning in a Thibodeaux, Louisiana, eatery. We traded a Pedernales River Chili recipe for it. Bean Chili a la Thibodeaux represents a delightful variation on traditional chili, and it's one we enjoy on cold winter nights.

1	pound dried beans (The Louisiana recipe called for red beans, but we have found pinto beans work well also.)
2	tablespoons olive oil
2	onions, chopped
2	garlic cloves, minced
1	stalk celery, chopped
3-4	fresh chile peppers, stemmed, seeded, and chopped (The Louisiana recipe used cayenne peppers, which were delicious. We substituted jalapeños with positive results. Other chiles, such as serranos, can also be used.)
2	tablespoons cumin
1	14½-ounce can crushed tomatoes
4	tomato cans of water
½	cup fresh cilantro, chopped
1	teaspoon oregano

Salt and pepper to taste

Place beans in a cooking pot, cover with water, and bring to boil for five to ten minutes, then set aside. After one hour, dump beans into a colander, drain, and rinse. Allow them to dry a bit in the sink while you work on other stuff. In a large cast-iron skillet, heat oil, add onions, garlic, celery, and chile peppers, and sauté. Add cumin, stir, and cook another two minutes. Add beans, tomatoes, water, cilantro, oregano, salt, and pepper; stir and bring to boil. Reduce heat to low and allow to simmer until beans are tender enough to eat, approximately two to two-and-a-half hours. Serve over rice and garnish with parsley and Tabasco sauce.

Black Bean Vegetarian Chili

The following is yet another variation on bean-based, meatless chili.

2   cups black beans
2   Anaheim chile peppers, stemmed, seeded, and peeled
2   tablespoons olive oil
2   medium onions, chopped
2   garlic cloves, minced
1   stalk celery, chopped
2   tablespoons chili powder
2   teaspoons cumin
2   teaspoons oregano
1   28-ounce can tomatoes, crushed
Salt and pepper to taste
½   cup parsley
½   cup green onions
¼   cup fresh cilantro, chopped

After soaking beans overnight in salted water, drain, rinse, place in large cooking pot, cover with fresh cold water, and bring to boil. Reduce heat and let simmer. Cut Anaheim chile peppers in half, place in shallow bowl, cover with boiling water, stir, and allow to set for forty-five minutes. Heat olive oil in skillet and sauté onions, garlic, and celery. Stir in chili powder, cumin, and oregano, and cook for another two minutes. When finished, place in pot with beans. Transfer the Anaheims to a blender, add one-half cup of the tomatoes, and puree. Add puree to pot, along with the remaining tomatoes. Continue to simmer for approximately one-and-a-half to two hours or until beans are tender, adding salt and pepper as you go. Serve topped with fresh chopped parsley, green onions, and cilantro.

Chicken Breast and White Bean Chili

This recipe is filled with nutritious low-calorie and low-cholesterol ingredients.

2 cups white beans
2 tablespoons chili powder
1 teaspoon cumin
1 teaspoon oregano
1 teaspoon cayenne
1 teaspoon thyme
3-4 chicken breasts, skinned, boned, and cubed
2 tablespoons olive oil
1 onion, chopped
2 garlic cloves, minced
1 stalk celery, chopped
2 cups chicken broth
4 ancho chile peppers, stemmed, seeded, peeled, and chopped

Salt and pepper to taste

Soak beans overnight, drain, place in pot and cover with fresh, cold water. Bring to boil, reduce heat, and simmer. In a bowl, mix chili powder, cumin, oregano, cayenne, and thyme. Add chicken and toss, making certain each cube of meat is well coated with the spices. In a large skillet, heat oil, add onion, garlic, and celery, and sauté. Place sautéed vegetables into the pot of beans. Add more oil to skillet if necessary, add chicken, and cook until meat is browned, stirring occasionally. Place chicken into pot of beans, add chicken broth and chopped anchos, stir, and allow to simmer for one-and-a-half to two hours or until beans are tender. If liquid is needed, add more chicken broth. Adjust for seasoning, and serve topped with chopped parsley.

Easy Black Bean Chili

This simple recipe takes only minutes to prepare.

2 tablespoons olive oil
1 large onion, chopped
2 garlic cloves, minced
2 15-ounce cans black beans
2-3 cups chicken broth
Salt and pepper to taste
1 tablespoon cumin

Heat oil in cooking pot, add onion and garlic, and sauté. Add beans, chicken broth, salt, and pepper; bring to boil, reduce heat, and let simmer for one-half hour. Add cumin, stir, and cook for additional ten minutes. Serve over rice and top with chopped green onions.

Eggplant Chili

This recipe, which substitutes eggplant for meat, is surprisingly delicious.

3 medium eggplants, cut into 3/4-inch slices
Salt, pepper, and paprika to taste
4-6 tablespoons olive oil
2 onions, chopped
2 garlic cloves, minced
4 fresh ancho or Anaheim chile peppers, stemmed, seeded, and chopped
4 tablespoons chili powder
3-4 tomatoes, chopped
2 green bell peppers, chopped
¼ cup tomato paste
1 tablespoon oregano
1 tablespoon thyme

After coating eggplant slices with olive oil, sprinkle with salt, pepper, and paprika, and grill over medium heat for no more than ten minutes, turning often. Remove from grill and set aside. In a cooking pot, heat oil and sauté onions, garlic, and chile peppers. Reduce heat slightly, add chili powder, stir, and cook for an additional two minutes. Add tomatoes, bell peppers, tomato paste, oregano, thyme, salt, pepper, and paprika; stir and cook for ten minutes. Cut eggplant slices into one-inch pieces, add to mix, and cook for another five minutes. Rice makes an excellent accompaniment to this dish, either on the side or with the chili poured on top. A dry white wine is an excellent complement to this dish.

Garbanzo and Pinto Bean Chili

For a meatless chili, this one packs a lot of flavor and exciting texture. Feel free to substitute kidney beans for pinto beans if you desire.

1½ cups dried garbanzos
1½ cups dried pinto beans
2   tablespoons olive oil
1   large onion, chopped
3   garlic cloves, minced
1   stalk celery, chopped
1   15-ounce can crushed tomatoes
1   8-ounce can tomato sauce
4   ancho chile peppers, stemmed, seeded, peeled, and chopped
2   tablespoons chili powder
2   teaspoons cumin
2   teaspoons oregano
2   serrano chile peppers, finely chopped
Salt to taste

Soak pinto and garbanzo beans overnight in salted water, drain, place in cooking pot, and cover with fresh, cold water. Bring to boil, reduce heat, and let simmer. Heat oil in cast-iron skillet and sauté onion, garlic, and celery. Add to beans along with tomatoes, tomato sauce, anchos, chili powder, cumin, and oregano. Stir and let simmer for another one-and-a-half hours or until beans are tender. Add liquid if necessary and adjust for seasoning. Fifteen minutes before serving, add serrano peppers and stir. Serve topped with fresh chopped cilantro or green onion.

Garden Chili

The following recipe was the result of the work of a committee. Several of us with home gardens pooled out harvest and responded to the challenge of preparing a vegetarian chili. The result is quite tasty.

2	tablespoons olive oil
1	large onion, chopped
1	green bell pepper, chopped
1	cup mushrooms, chopped
4	fresh jalapeño peppers, minced
3	tablespoons chili powder
1	tablespoon oregano
1	teaspoon cumin
2	cups water
½	cup uncooked cracked wheat
2	14½-ounce cans diced tomatoes (Use fresh garden tomatoes if you have them, but be sure to remove the peels)
1	10-ounce can tomato puree
1	cup corn
2	16-ounce cans white beans

Heat oil in a large cooking pot; add onion, bell pepper, mushrooms, jalapeños, chili powder, oregano, and cumin, and sauté. Add water, cracked wheat, tomatoes, and tomato puree. Stir, bring to boil, reduce heat, and let simmer for thirty minutes. Add corn and beans, cook for another ten minutes, and serve. Garnish with fresh chopped parsley or cilantro.

Healthy Chicken Chili

Another one of our favorite low-calorie recipes.

2   tablespoons olive oil
1   pound chicken, cubed
1   large onion, chopped
1   green bell pepper, chopped
1-2 jalapeños, chopped
½   cup sun-dried tomatoes
2   tablespoons chili powder
1   tablespoon cumin
2   teaspoons oregano
3   garlic cloves, minced
2   cups water
1   cup pinto beans, dried
2   large fresh tomatoes, peeled and chopped
1   cup corn (fresh is preferred but canned will do)
Salt and ground red pepper to taste

In a large cooking pot, heat oil, add chicken and onion, and cook for two to three minutes. Add bell pepper, jalapeños, dried tomatoes, chili powder, cumin, oregano, and garlic and cook over medium heat for one to two minutes. Add water and dried beans, bring to boil, cover, and reduce heat; let simmer for one to two hours, or until beans are tender. Add fresh tomatoes, corn, salt, and pepper; stir well, return to boil, and cook for additional five to ten minutes, then serve.

Low-Fat Texas Chili with Beef

The use of a small amount of lean beef in this low-cal recipe provides a burst of great taste.

1	tablespoon olive oil
½	pound very lean sirloin
1	large onion, chopped
1	green bell pepper, chopped
1	8-ounce can tomato sauce
1	13½-ounce can beef broth
1	6-ounce can tomato paste
1-2	tablespoons chili powder
1	teaspoon cumin
2	16-ounce cans pinto beans

In a large cast-iron skillet heat oil and brown beef. Add onion and green pepper and cook over medium heat until beef is done. Drain. Add tomato sauce, beef broth, tomato paste, chili powder, cumin, and beans; stir well and simmer for at least one hour. Adjust seasonings to taste.

Mushroom Chili

More and more we are encountering vegetarian friends who substitute mushrooms for meat on a regular basis. Some portobello burgers we've consumed lately have been incredibly delicious, and several different varieties of meatless pasta sauce made with mushrooms have likewise been delectable. It was only a matter of time before someone experimented with mushrooms in chili. With the help of several adventurous chiliheads, we offer the following recipe.

4   tablespoons olive oil
4   onions, chopped
4   garlic cloves, minced
4   tablespoons chili powder
1   tablespoon cumin
3   pound fresh mushrooms, chopped
2   green or red bell peppers, chopped
½   cup tomato paste
2   tablespoons dried leaf oregano
1   tablespoon dried leaf basil
Salt and black pepper to taste

In a cooking pot, heat olive oil, add onions and garlic, and sauté. Add chili powder and cumin, stir, and cook for another minute. Add mushrooms and cook over medium heat for approximately fifteen minutes. Add bell peppers, tomato paste, oregano, basil, salt, and pepper; mix well and cook for another ten minutes. If more liquid is needed, add tomato juice or beer. If a thicker chili is desired, add a paste made from masa harina and water.

Peak of Health Vegetarian Chili

Vegetarian chilis offer the challenge of maintaining a chili taste without the use of meat. The following recipe offers an excellent blend of vegetables and spices to yield a delicious chili that, for vegetarian, packs a wallop.

2-3 cups pinto beans, soaked overnight in water
2-3 teaspoons salt
2 tablespoons olive oil
2 onions, chopped
4 garlic cloves, minced
3 stalks celery, chopped
3 carrots, chopped
4 tomatoes, peeled
6 tablespoons chili powder
1 teaspoon cumin
½ teaspoon oregano
1 teaspoon basil
½-1 teaspoon ground black pepper
1-2 green bell peppers, chopped
1 cup tomato juice
1 cup cracked wheat

Drain pinto beans, transfer to cooking pot, cover with fresh water, add one teaspoon salt, and bring to a boil. Let boil for one minute, lower the heat to simmer, and cook beans until tender, approximately one to two hours. Heat olive oil in large pot, add onions and garlic, and sauté. When onions are translucent, add celery, carrots, tomatoes, and the remaining spices and salt. Cover pot and cook over medium heat for fifteen minutes or until vegetables are tender. Add bell peppers and cook another ten minutes. In a separate saucepan, bring tomato juice to a boil. Remove from heat, add cracked wheat, stir, and let sit for five minutes. Add pinto beans (with their water) and cracked wheat, stir well, and simmer for another thirty minutes. Add water if needed, and adjust seasonings for taste.

Poor Man's Vegetarian Chili

Lorenzo Borrego, who provided this recipe, is a vegetarian who, as he claims, lives on a tight budget. Following years of trial and error, he has arrived at this recipe, which is inexpensive and quite nutritious. It is also very easy to make.

4-5   8-ounce cans tomato sauce
1   6-ounce can tomato paste
1   cup mushrooms, chopped
1   red bell pepper, chopped
2-3   jalapeño peppers, diced
1   onion, chopped
Salt to taste
Crushed red pepper to taste
6   tablespoons chili powder
1   tablespoon cumin
2   garlic cloves, minced
1   teaspoon oregano
½   teaspoon allspice
1   cup textured soy protein

In a large cooking pot, combine tomato sauce, tomato paste, mushrooms, bell pepper, jalapeños, onion, salt, pepper, chili powder, cumin, garlic, oregano, and allspice. Stir thoroughly, add soy, and bring to boil. Allow to boil for one minute, lower heat, and simmer for one-and-a-half to two hours. Serve with sourdough bread and iced tea.

Shitake and White Mushroom Chili

The blend of shitake and white mushrooms offers something quite different from most of the recipes found in this section.

2	tablespoons olive oil
1	large onion, chopped
2	garlic cloves, minced
3	tablespoons chili powder
1	teaspoon cumin
½	pound fresh shitake mushrooms, chopped
1½	pounds fresh white mushrooms, chopped
1	14½-ounce can stewed tomatoes
1	19-ounce can white beans, drained

In a large cooking pot, heat olive oil, add onion and garlic, and sauté. Add chili powder and cumin and cook for additional minute or two, stirring frequently. Add mushrooms and cook for another six or seven minutes. Add tomatoes and beans and about one-half cup of water. Stir and let simmer for additional ten minutes. Serve topped with fresh chopped parsley or cilantro.

Skinny Minnie Chili

Minnie Mendoza claims she lost eighty-three pounds eating nothing but one serving of this chili per day over a six-week period.

2 tablespoons olive oil
1 large onion, chopped
½ stalk celery, chopped
1 green bell pepper, chopped
½ cup mushrooms, sliced
2 pounds boneless chicken breasts
3 tablespoons chili powder
½ teaspoon oregano
1 teaspoon cumin
3 garlic cloves, minced
Salt to taste
1 16-ounce can tomatoes
1 6-ounce can tomato paste
1 4-ounce can green chiles

Heat oil in cooking pot, add onion, celery, and bell pepper, and sauté. Add mushrooms and cook for additional five minutes. Add chicken, chili powder, oregano, cumin, and garlic; stir well and cook until meat is browned nicely. Add remaining ingredients, bring to boil, reduce heat, and allow to simmer for one to one-and-a-half hours, stirring occasionally.

Slim's Diet Chili

Slim was a West Texas cowhand who professed to love chili more than life itself. "A day without chili ain't nothin' to look forward to," Slim often said. After Slim's weight ballooned to over 250 pounds on his five-foot, seven-inch frame, he started cutting down on portions of chili and experimented with leaner ingredients. The result follows, and the total calories count is less than 250 per bowl.

1	tablespoon olive oil
2	onions, chopped
1	garlic clove, minced
1½-2	pounds very lean beef, coarsely ground
3	tablespoons chili powder
1	teaspoon Mexican oregano
1-2	teaspoons cumin
	Salt to taste
4-5	fresh tomatoes, peeled and chopped
3-4	4-ounce cans chopped green chiles

Heat oil in large cast-iron skillet, add onions and garlic, and sauté. Add meat, chili powder, oregano, cumin, and salt; stir well and cook until meat is browned. Add tomatoes and green chiles and a bit of water, bring to boil, lower heat, then simmer for at least one hour, stirring occasionally and adding water if necessary. Let sit overnight in refrigerator. When ready to serve, skim any congealed grease off top, heat, and serve.

Salt-Free Chili

For those who must remain cautious about their salt intake, the following recipe deserves a try.

1   tablespoon olive oil
3   medium onions, chopped
1   green bell pepper, chopped
1-1½ pounds veal, cubed
2   garlic cloves, minced
2   tablespoons ground red chile, hot
1   tablespoon ground red chile, mild
1   teaspoon cumin
1   teaspoon oregano
½   teaspoon black pepper
4   cups canned tomatoes (may use fresh, if available)
1   tablespoon red wine vinegar

Heat oil in a cast-iron skillet, add onions and bell pepper, and sauté. When onions are translucent, add veal, garlic, chiles, cumin, and oregano, stirring well. When meat is browned, add pepper, tomatoes, and vinegar. Allow to simmer for at least one hour, stirring occasionally. Add seasonings for taste, if desired.

Soybean Chili #1

Soybeans are making serious inroads into all kinds of recipes. It was inevitable they would find their way into the chili pot.

1	tablespoon olive oil
2	medium onions, chopped
5-6	garlic cloves, minced
1	14½-ounce can chopped tomatoes
1	tablespoon oregano
1	tablespoon cumin
1	tablespoon chili powder
2	cups cooked soybeans

Heat olive oil in skillet and sauté onions and garlic for about five minutes. Lower heat slightly, add tomatoes, and cook for additional five minutes. Add oregano, cumin, and chili powder; stir well and cook for another three minutes. Add soybeans, bring to boil, then reduce heat and allow to simmer for forty-five minutes.

Soybean Chili #2

This recipe is the result of a couple of years of tinkering with ingredients, combinations of same, tasting, and experimenting on friends.

2 tablespoon olive oil
2 teaspoons cumin
2 medium onions, chopped
6-8 ounces tempeh,* chopped
1 tablespoon minced garlic
1 green bell pepper, diced
1 red bell pepper, diced
2 tablespoons chili powder
2 teaspoons oregano
3 ancho chiles, stemmed, seeded, and finely chopped
1 bottle beer, preferably Mexican
2 cans tomatoes, chopped
2 cups cooked soybeans
Salt to taste
3-4 tablespoons fresh cilantro, chopped

Heat oil in skillet, add cumin, and sauté for a few seconds. Add onions and tempeh and sauté until onions are translucent. Add garlic, bell peppers, chili powder, oregano, and chile peppers, and sauté for another one to two minutes, stirring constantly. Add beer, tomatoes, and soybeans; bring to boil, cover, reduce heat, and allow to simmer for one-half hour. Before serving, add cilantro and stir well.

* Tempeh is a soybean product that can be found in good health food stores.

Texas Penicillin

This recipe, provided by editor and writer Ginnie Bivona, is called Texas Penicillin because it is "a sure cure for everything, including broken hearts."

2	pounds boneless chicken breasts, cubed
4	cans low-salt chicken stock
1	14-ounce can Italian-style diced tomatoes
3	garlic cloves, finely chopped
1	medium zucchini, sliced thinly
1	medium carrot, sliced thinly
1	large red pepper, diced
1	14-ounce can sweet corn
1	15-ounce can Ranch Style beans
2-3	tablespoons chili powder
1½-2	tablespoons cumin
4	green onions, sliced
½	cup fresh cilantro, chopped

Place chicken in large pot with chicken stock, tomatoes, and garlic. Bring to boil, reduce heat, and simmer for twenty minutes. Add all fresh vegetables and simmer for additional ten minutes. Add canned vegetables and remaining spices and simmer another ten minutes. Remove from heat, add green onions and cilantro, and serve with crusty bread and a mixed green salad with honey mustard dressing.

Vegetarian Chili No. 1

The following is one of the simplest and quickest recipes in this entire book.

3   cups water
2   15½-ounce cans Ranch Style beans
1   14½-ounce can diced tomatoes
1   11½-ounce can Snap-E-Tom tomato juice
1   medium onion, chopped
1   4½-ounce can chopped green chiles
½   cup uncooked long grain rice
2   teaspoons cumin

In a large cooking pot, combine all ingredients, bring to boil, reduce to low heat, cover, and allow to cook for at least twenty minutes or until rice is done.

Vegetarian Chili #2

1-2 tablespoons cooking oil
2 garlic cloves, minced
2 tablespoons chili powder
1 teaspoon cumin
½ teaspoon oregano
½ teaspoon black pepper
2 cups green beans
2-3 carrots, finely chopped
4-5 stalks celery, chopped
1 15-ounce can tomatoes
1 cup water
1 onion, chopped
2 green or red bell peppers, chopped
2 New Mexico green chiles, peeled and chopped
1 can pinto beans
Salt to taste

In a large cooking pot, heat oil, add garlic, chili powder, cumin, oregano, and pepper, and cook for two minutes. Add green beans, carrots, celery, tomatoes, and water. Bring to boil and simmer for fifteen minutes. Add onion, bell peppers, green chiles, and pinto beans and cook an additional ten to fifteen minutes. Adjust seasonings to taste.

Vegetarian Chili with Chicken

1 tablespoon olive oil

1 pound boned, skinned, and cubed chicken, preferably white meat

1 onion, chopped

1 green bell pepper, chopped

2-3 jalapeño peppers, chopped

2-3 garlic cloves, minced

¼ cup sun-dried tomatoes

2 tablespoons chili powder

1 tablespoon cumin

2 teaspoons oregano

Salt and pepper to taste

2 cups water

1 cup dried pinto beans, soaked overnight in saltwater, drained

1 cup fresh tomato, chopped

1 cup fresh corn

In a skillet heat oil and brown chicken. Add onion, bell pepper, jalapeños, and garlic, and sauté. Add tomatoes, chili powder, cumin, oregano, salt, and pepper. Stir well and cook for one minute. Add water and beans, stir again, bring to boil, reduce heat, and let simmer for an hour and a half. Add fresh tomato and corn and continue simmering another thirty minutes or until pinto beans are tender.

Vegetarian Chili with a Zing

The addition of lots of jalapeño peppers along with spicy Bloody Mary mix gives this version of chili an extra zing.

1   cup spicy Bloody Mary mix
1   cup cracked wheat
2   tablespoons olive oil
2   medium onions, chopped
2   garlic cloves, minced
2   stalks celery, chopped
4-6 tablespoons chili powder
1   teaspoon oregano
1   28-ounce can tomatoes, crushed
2   cups water
2   green or red bell peppers
4-5 jalapeño peppers
2   packages frozen green beans
2   cans pinto beans, drained
2   cans garbanzos, drained
1   can corn, drained
Salt, black pepper, and cayenne pepper to taste

Allow cracked wheat to soak in Bloody Mary mix for one hour. Heat oil in large cooking pot, add onions, garlic, and celery, and sauté. Add chili powder, oregano, tomatoes, and water. Stir, bring to boil, reduce heat, and allow to simmer for one-half hour. Add bell peppers and jalapeños and cook for another fifteen to twenty minutes. Add green beans and cracked wheat, stir, and cook additional twenty minutes, stirring frequently. Add pinto beans, garbanzos, and corn, and cook another fifteen minutes. Add salt and pepper to taste and serve.

Wheat Chili

"**W**heat, not meat," claims a chili-loving friend who came up with the following recipe in response to a doctor's order to lose fifty pounds. In spite of the title, this recipe contains one pound of lean meat. Aside from the addition of whole wheat kernels, this recipe contains, for the most part, many of the traditional ingredients expected in a great bowl of chili.

1	cup whole wheat kernels
2	tablespoons olive oil
2	onions, chopped
1	pound very lean beef, cubed
3-4	tablespoons chili powder
3	garlic cloves, minced
½	teaspoon oregano
2	teaspoons cumin

Salt to taste

½	teaspoon crushed red pepper
1	8-ounce can green chiles
1	8-ounce can tomato paste
1	32-ounce can tomato juice

Wheat kernels can be purchased at most health food stores. Soak the kernels overnight in water. The next day, place the wheat, along with the water in which it soaked, into a saucepan and bring to a boil. Heat oil in large skillet, add onions, and sauté. In a separate bowl, combine beef, chili powder, garlic, oregano, cumin, and salt. Mix well, add to skillet, stir, and cook until meat is browned. Add red pepper, green chiles, tomato paste, and tomato juice. Drain wheat and save liquid. Add wheat to skillet and stir, bring to boil, reduce heat, and allow to simmer for one hour. Add some of the liquid when necessary. Serve with tossed green salad.

Celebrity Recipes

*T*his section features chili recipes from a variety of celebrities ranging from writers, singers, songwriters, actors, and noted chiliheads. Over the years, we have noted there exists a passion for the cooking and eating of chili among writers, performers, and other celebrities, therefore, we decided to include a few of our favorites here.

Gunsmoke Chili
James Arness

4-5 pounds ground beef or venison
4-5 medium onions, chopped
4-5 tablespoons chili powder
1   4-ounce can green chile peppers, chopped
1   15-ounce can tomatoes, chopped
1-2 tablespoons cumin
1-2 tablespoons ground coriander
1-2 tablespoons red pepper
2   jalapeño peppers, chopped
2   15-ounce cans chili beans
¼   cup Pace picante sauce, hot
3   cups water
2   tablespoons lime juice
½   can beer

Brown meat in large Dutch oven. Add remaining ingredients and cook, covered, for four hours. Add water, if needed.

Noted actor James Arness is best known for his role as Marshall Matt Dillon on television's *Gunsmoke*.

"Sound the Alarm" Texas Red Chili
Frederic Bean

"*Not for the faint of heart,*" *says Bean.*

2	lbs. whole chuck or rump roast cut into 2-inch squares
16	ounces water
½	white onion, diced
⅓	cup ancho red chili powder
1	tablespoon dried garlic pieces
1	teaspoon paprika
1	teaspoon red pepper
1	teaspoon cumin
1	teaspoon salt
1	8-ounce can tomato sauce
1	tablespoon masa harina

Place diced meat, onion, and one tablespoon of chili powder in a crock pot along with 4 ounces of water. Cover and cook on "high" for four to five hours or until meat is very tender. (Note: Crock pot settings vary by manufacturer; use the heat setting recommended for your crock pot.) Add the rest of the chili powder, garlic, paprika, red pepper, cumin, salt, tomato sauce, and the remaining water. Cover and stir occasionally for one more hour. Mix masa harina in small amount of water and add to pot, stir, and cook another half-hour.

Serve with large glasses of ice water or very cold Tecate beer. Dessert must be ice cream.

Frederic Bean is the author of forty western, historical, and mystery novels, and the co-author of the nonfiction book *The Return of the Outlaw Billy the Kid*. He lives in Belton, Texas.

Longhorn Chili
Kent Biffle

Noted newspaper columnist Biffle's recipe is unique in that it calls for the beef from a longhorn!

2 pounds coarsely ground longhorn beef
2 pork sausage patties
2 10-ounce cans Rotel diced tomatoes with chile peppers, lime, and cilantro
1 11 ½-ounce can tomato juice
2 tablespoons cumin
4-6 tablespoons chili powder
1 cup onions, chopped
Garlic powder to taste
Oregano to taste
1 pot of coffee

Brown the beef in a big pot and drain. Add sausages and cook until crumbly. Add tomatoes, tomato juice, cumin, chili powder, onions, garlic powder, and oregano and stir. Simmer for a couple of hours, adding coffee when liquid is needed. Texture of chili can be adjusted just before serving by adding a spoonful or two of paste made from masa harina and water.

The result, according to Biffle, is a "spicy long-horn chili as tender as a maiden's kiss."

Kent Biffle is a former *Newsweek* correspondent, author of two books, and is perhaps best known for his immensely popular "Texana" column in the *Dallas Morning News*. He lives in Rockwall, Texas.

Terlingua Creek Yacht Club and Marina Chili
Ginnie Bivona

2 tablespoons olive oil
3 pounds chuck, cut into small cubes
1 small yellow onion, finely chopped
2 medium garlic cloves, minced
2 small cans Contadina tomato sauce
2 cans Swanson's beef stock
9 tablespoons Gebhardt chili powder
3 tablespoons cumin
2 fresh jalapeños, seeded and finely chopped
⅛ teaspoon cayenne pepper
Salt to taste
Water as needed

In a well-aged cast-iron skillet, heat oil and brown meat until all the pink color is gone. Add onion and garlic, cook a few minutes, then add tomato sauce and enough beef stock to cover the meat. Bring to a boil, reduce heat, add three tablespoons chili powder, and allow to simmer for one hour. Add three more tablespoons chili powder, cumin, jalapeños, and more beef stock if needed. Continue to simmer, and after another hour add the remainder of the chili powder, cayenne, and more cumin (if desired). Add water if necessary. Salt to taste and simmer for yet another hour or until meat is very tender and gravy is thick.

Ginnie Bivona is a writer, is employed in the publishing industry, and is a veteran contestant of Texas chili cook-offs.

Doc Blakely's Fuego de Tejas (Fire of Texas) Chili #13
Doc Blakely

2½ pounds sirloin, cubed
½ pound ground sausage
4 tablespoons regular chili powder
3 tablespoons hot chili powder
1 teaspoon garlic powder
¾ teaspoon red cayenne pepper
1 can tomato sauce
1 cup onion, finely chopped
2 tablespoons ground cumin
¼ teaspoon oregano, dried
10 ounces beef broth
Salt, pepper, and water to taste

Combine beef and sausage, brown well in cast-iron pot, and drain. While meat is browning, combine chili powders, garlic powder, and cayenne in small bowl and mix well. Sprinkle three-fourths of this mixture on the browned meat and reserve remainder for later. Add tomato sauce and onion. Stir in cumin and oregano. Cover and simmer for two hours until meat is almost done, adding water or dark beer as needed to keep meat just barely covered. Add remaining spice mixture, stir well, and cover and simmer for another one-half hour until thick. Salt and pepper to taste. Serve with side order of sliced jalapeño peppers.

Blakely maintains this recipe serves ten normal people or five Texans!

Doc Blakely—humorist, entertainer, musician, and author of seven books—is one of the country's most sought-after conference and convention speakers.

Uncle Roger's Quien Sabe Chili
Mike Blakely

3-4 pounds venison
2 pounds pork, freshly ground
1-2 pounds round steak, cubed
½ cup bacon drippings
2 8-ounce cans tomato sauce
1 tablespoon Tabasco sauce
½ teaspoon cayenne pepper
2 14-ounce cans tomatoes, peeled
1 teaspoon paprika
1 tablespoon oregano
1 tablespoon cumin
1 teaspoon dry mustard
1 bottle burgundy wine
3 cloves garlic, chopped
3 onions, chopped
6 tablespoons chili powder
1 tablespoon salt

In a cast-iron pot, brown the meats, add bacon drippings, and cook for five minutes. Add tomato sauce, Tabasco sauce, cayenne, and peeled tomatoes and simmer for thirty minutes, adding water as needed. Add remaining ingredients and simmer for additional one to two hours. If a thicker chili is desired, mix a paste of water and flour and add.

Native Texan Mike Blakely is a novelist and has written over ten books. When he is not writing and hanging out at his *Rancho Quien Sabe*, he is a professional musician and songwriter, specializing in authentic cowboy ballads. He performs regularly from coast to coast and has appeared in Australia and Italy.

Venison Chili
Lawrence Clayton

5 pounds venison, coarsely ground
½ pound beef suet
1 large onion, minced
10 tablespoons chili powder
1 tablespoon salt
1 #2 can tomato juice
pepper and garlic to taste

Brown venison in suet in large cast-iron pot and drain excess grease. Cover with water and bring to boil. Add onion and seasonings and allow to simmer over low heat for approximately three hours. Add tomato juice thirty minutes before serving. If extra fire is desired for taste, add a few chopped jalapeño peppers.

Lawrence Clayton is the author of several books and articles about cowboys and ranch history and serves as Professor of English and Dean of the College of Arts and Sciences at Hardin-Simmons University in Abilene, Texas. He and his wife, Sonja, operate their J Lazy C Ranch in Throckmorton County just north of old Fort Griffin.

Don's Chili
Don Coldsmith

1	pound ground beef
1	pound cubed beef
1	large onion, chopped
1	green bell pepper, chopped
1	4-ounce can green chiles, chopped
3	15-ounce cans tomatoes, chopped
2	15-ounce cans red beans
2-3	tablespoons chili powder
½	teaspoon salt
½	teaspoon cinnamon
½	teaspoon cumin
½	teaspoon oregano
½	teaspoon garlic powder
¼	teaspoon cloves
¼	teaspoon black pepper

Brown beef, drain, add onion and bell pepper and cook lightly. Add other ingredients and simmer two to three hours.

For variety, other meats such as venison or pork can be substituted.

Don Coldsmith is the award-winning author of over thirty books, 150 magazine articles, and over 1,300 newspaper columns. Coldsmith is perhaps best known for his incredibly successful series of historical novels, the "Spanish Bit Saga" about the Indians of the Great Plains. There are over six million copies of Coldsmith's books in print.

In addition to being a fine novelist, Coldsmith has also been a minister, gunsmith, taxidermist, disc jockey, picolo player, and grain inspector. Coldsmith was one of the last mule packers ever used by the U.S. Army.

Joe Cooper's Chili
Joe E. Cooper

Regarded by many during his time as a chili guru, Joe Cooper provided many of us with important information, inspiration, and entertainment.

3	pounds lean beef
¼	cup olive oil
1	quart water
2	bay leaves (optional)
6	tablespoons chili powder
3	teaspoons salt
10	garlic cloves, minced
1	teaspoon cumin
1	teaspoon oregano
1	teaspoon red pepper
½	teaspoon black pepper
1	tablespoon sugar
3	tablespoons paprika
3	tablespoons flour
6	tablespoons cornmeal

Heat oil in large pot, add meat, and cook until grey. Add one quart water and allow to simmer for one-and-a-half to two hours. Add remaining ingredients except for flour and cornmeal and simmer for another thirty minutes. Add flour and corneal to desired thickness, stirring often.

The late Joe E. Cooper, the author of *With Or Without Beans*, can rightfully be considered a celebrity, and one that was well known to the world's chiliheads. To many, Cooper's book remains essential reading on the subject of chili.

Southwest Territory Chili
James A. Crutchfield

2   large onions, chopped
2   pounds ground beef
2   large cans chopped tomatoes
3   cans kidney or pinto beans
¼   cup barbecue sauce
2   tablespoons chili powder
1   package chili mix
Salt to taste

In a large cast-iron skillet, sauté onions. Add meat and brown. Add remaining ingredients, lower heat, and simmer for at least two hours. Serve topped with cheddar cheese and/or Fritos corn chips.

James A. Crutchfield is an award-winning historian and writer who makes his home in Franklin, Tennessee. The author of thirty nonfiction books and hundreds of magazine and newspaper articles, he has also written for television. Crutchfield serves as Secretary-Treasurer for the Western Writers of America, Inc.

E. DeGolyer's Recipe
(E. DeGolyer)

*J*oe Cooper described the late E. DeGolyer as a "world-traveler gourmet." Cookbook author
Jane Trahey called him "Texas' Solomon of the chili bowl."

2½ cups rendered fat from beef suet
1   onion, chopped
4   cloves garlic, chopped
3   pounds center cut steak, trimmed and cubed
2   cups water
1   teaspoon cumin
1   teaspoon oregano
4   tablespoons chili powder
1   tablespoon salt

Heat fat in cast-iron skillet and sauté onion and garlic. Add meat and brown. Cover with water and let simmer for one hour. Add cumin, oregano, chili powder, and salt, stir, and simmer on another hour.

Chili Woody
Woodruff DeSilva

3   tablespoons cooking oil
5   medium onions, chopped
Salt and pepper to taste
4   pounds beef chuck, cubed
5   garlic cloves, minced
4   tablespoons Mexican oregano
8   tablespoons chili powder
2   tablespoons paprika
2   teaspoons woodruff
1   teaspoon cayenne
1   teaspoon chile pequins, crushed
4   dashes Tabasco sauce
3   8-ounce cans tomato sauce
1   6-ounce can tomato paste
Water
¼   cup masa harina

In a large skillet, heat oil, add onions, salt, and pepper, and sauté until onions are browned. Add meat and cook until gray, at which point you add garlic and oregano, stirring occasionally. Mix together the remaining seasonings and chiles, add to meat, and stir well while simmering. Add Tabasco sauce, tomato sauce, and tomato paste, cover, and continue to simmer for another two hours, adding water when necessary.

DeSilva, like many serious chili chefs, insists the chili be placed in the refrigerator overnight to allow the flavors of the different ingredients to meld. Reheat the next day, and if a thicker chili is desired, add a bit of paste made from water and masa harina.

Woody DeSilva was once the manager of the Los Angeles International Airport. This recipe won the second annual International Chili Society's World Championship cook-off held in Terlingua, Texas, in 1968.

Cadillac Chili
Loren D. Estleman

Antoine de la Mothe, Seur de Cadillac, was the great explorer who founded Detroit, the setting of many of Estleman's crime and mystery novels. At the time, what is now the state of Michigan was regarded as the western frontier, yet another setting for Estleman's western novels.

2	pounds ground round steak
3	40-ounce cans dark red kidney beans
3	1.25-ounce packages McCormick Chili Seasoning
4	large tomatoes, diced
1	green bell pepper, chopped
1	sweet red pepper, chopped
1	12-ounce can beer
1	cup sour cream
1	whole bay leaf
1	tablespoon nutmeg

Brown meat in large pot or skillet, add other ingredients, stir, and simmer for four to five hours. According to Estleman, whoever winds up with the bay leaf in his bowl will be the recipient of good luck.

Loren D. Estleman is the critically acclaimed author of over forty novels. He is the recipient of three Shamus Awards from the Private Eye Writers of America, three Spur Awards from the Western Writers of America, and has been nominated for the Pulitzer Prize, the National Book Award, and the Mystery Writers of America Edgar Award.

Wick Fowler's 2-Alarm Chili
Wick Fowler

Some claim Wick Fowler is to Texas chili what Willie Nelson is to Texas music. Such important considerations are always arguable and probably best left to philosophers to debate. Regardless of Fowler's ranking among the world's most noted chili cooks, the truth remains that he makes one heck of a fine bowl of chili.

2	tablespoons vegetable oil
2	pounds diced beef
1	8-ounce can tomato sauce
2	cups water
3	tablespoons New Mexico chile powder
1	tablespoon paprika
1	teaspoon oregano
1	teaspoon cumin
1	teaspoon dehydrated garlic
1	teaspoon salt
1	teaspoon cayenne

In a large cast-iron skillet, brown beef in cooking oil and drain. Add tomato sauce, water, and seasonings, stir well, cover, and simmer for one hour and fifteen minutes. Skim off any grease. If a thicker chili is desired, make a paste with some masa harina and water and add to mix.

Wick Fowler's recipe for 2-Alarm Chili won first place at the Fourth Annual World Championship Chili Cookoff in 1970 at Terlingua, Texas.

Buffalo Chili Verde
Kathleen and Michael Gear

3   pounds buffalo shoulder roast
1   pound buffalo marrow bones
48   ounces canned tomatoes
23   ounces tomato sauce
4   garlic cloves, diced
28   ounces chicken broth
21   ounces Ortega green chile strips, diced
6   jalapeños, diced
½   cup dark beer
Salt and pepper to taste
1   teaspoon cumin seeds
1   teaspoon coriander seeds
1   bunch fresh cilantro, diced

Boil roast and cut into ½-inch thick cubes. Combine all other ingredients and allow to simmer for two hours. Remove marrow bones and serve.

Kathleen and Michael Gear are professional archeologists and anthropologists-turned-novelists. Collectively and individually, they have written two dozen novels including the best-selling *People of the Fire*, *People of the River*, and *People of the Earth*.

California Frontier Survival Chili '71
Ormly Gumfudgin

This recipe is known around the globe as chili cook-off champion Gumfudgin's low-calorie anti-smog chili. For the first time, Gumfudgin's secret ingredient is revealed.

5   pounds antelope rump roast marinated in California red wine

Safflower oil

4   cloves garlic, minced

2   Bermuda onions, finely chopped

1   cup bell pepper, chopped

1   stalk celery, chopped

20   ounces canned tomato puree

5   tablespoons Salsa Brava

2-3   cans beer

Large handful dried Oriental mushrooms

1½   small cans sliced water chestnuts

2   cans cocktail onions

½   teaspoon salt

1   teaspoon chili powder

1   tablespoon black pepper, freshly ground

2   teaspoons ground cumin

2   teaspoons ground oregano

2   teaspoons woodruff

2   tablespoons masa harina

½   cup wheat germ

½   cup kelp

1   pound white Mexican cheese

2   capsules each, vitamins E and A

Secret ingredient

For best results use fresh spices. Cover bottom of pot with oil and heat. Brown marinated meat for ten to fifteen minutes, adding oil if necessary. Add garlic, onions, bell pepper, and celery and brown together. Gently add 75 percent of Salsa Brava and allow a few minutes for penetration. Add remaining ingredients. After thirty minutes of cooking, taste and add rest of Salsa Brava, along with more chili powder, if desired. If water is needed to thin mixture, be sure to use only artesian spring water.

Just before serving, add Gumfudgin's secret ingredient—three pinches of gold flakes and stir briskly. Gumfudgin claimed he picked up this secret in Japan, where it is believed to relieve arthritis.

Ormly Gumfudgin has been a disc jockey, newscaster, actor, humorist, writer, newspaper columnist, chili cook-off consultant, chili judge, and one of the founders of the International Chili Society. Gumfudgin is famous as the world's only living bazooka player and has been honored for such in Ripley's Believe It Or Not. His hobbies are judging chili and spreading happiness.

Buckskin Beau Jacques' Mountain Man Chili
R.C. House

*"U*se a cast-iron skillet with a domed lid so the moisture can collect and drip back into the mix. Once you put the lid on for the final simmer leave it alone—too much peeking and stirring allows the flavors to escape."*

"Always stir with a wooden spoon."

1½ pounds beef flank steak
1½ pounds pork shoulder (or, if you wish, substitute beef heart)
4 large celery stalks chopped fine
1 large white onion chopped fine
1 large tomato peeled and chopped
1 large can tomato sauce
1 small can green chile salsa
1 teaspoon cumin
½ teaspoon garlic powder
1 teaspoon oregano
2 teaspoons chili powder
1 teaspoon cayenne
1 teaspoon Tabasco sauce
1 can beer
¼ cup masa harina

Debone meat if necessary, remove fat, and cut into one-inch cubes. Render small amount of fat in cast-iron Dutch oven, add meat, and brown over medium heat. Place all remaining ingredients except beer and masa harina into saucepan, cover, and cook for twenty minutes over low heat. When done, add to meat, stir, add beer, cover, and simmer for 2½ hours. If increased thickness is desired, mix masa with water to form a thin paste and add as much as needed.

R.C. House is the author of twelve western novels, an Old West collectibles guide, and hundreds of articles, columns, and book reviews.

Marty Robbins' Campfire Chili
Marty Robbins

This unorthodox chili recipe includes potatoes and eggs!

1   pound ground beef
1   medium onion, chopped
1   large potato, grated
2   teaspoons cumin
1-3 teaspoons ground red pepper
2   teaspoons oregano
6   eggs, beaten
Salt and pepper to taste
Vegetable oil (optional)

Brown the meat in large skillet and drain. Add onion, potato, and spices and stir well. To keep the mix from sticking, add a small amount of vegetable oil if necessary. When the potatoes are browned add the beaten eggs to the mixture. Stir until eggs are cooked.

The late Marty Robbins was an award-winning country and western performer and recording artist, a popular songwriter, and a successful race car driver.

Chili H. Allen Smith
H. Allen Smith

H. *Allen Smith had the temerity to chastise Texans for their reluctance to add beans and sweet peppers to chili, calling them "daft." In spite of the many enemies he made, Smith eventually moved from New York to Southwest Texas. Smith became a major contributor to the history and culture of chili.*

3	pounds lean chuck, round, or tenderloin, coarsely ground, and all fat removed
1-2	cans tomato paste
1-2	onions, chopped
½	bell pepper, chopped
2-3	garlic cloves, minced
½	teaspoon oregano
2	pinches sweet basil
¼	teaspoon cumin
2	tablespoons chili powder
Salt to taste	
1	can pinto or kidney beans

Sear meat in cast-iron kettle. Smith says, "If you don't have an iron kettle, you are not civilized; go out and get one." Add tomato paste, onions, bell pepper, and one quart water. Stir and simmer. Add garlic, oregano, basil, cumin, chili powder, and salt. Let simmer for one-and-a-half to two hours, adjusting seasonings to taste. When satisfied with the product, add a can of pinto or kidney beans and heat for a few more minutes. Remove from stove and allow to set overnight. Chili, according to Smith, always tastes better the second day.

Writer and columnist H. Allen Smith was the author of *The Great Chili Confrontation*, a hilarious, thigh-slapping book about an historic chili cook-off battle. The late Smith was the acknowledged and often-maligned champion for placing beans in chili.

Hallie's Chili
Hallie Stillwell

One of the joys of visiting the Big Bend area of Texas was the opportunity to spend some time with long-time resident Hallie Stillwell. Stillwell, who was considered a pioneer of the region, could be counted on to offer insight into wildlife, ranching, weather, and chili.

2	pounds venison, cubed
4	tablespoons olive oil
2	onions, chopped
4	garlic cloves, minced
1	14½-ounce can tomatoes
4	cups water
3	tablespoons Gebhardt's chili powder
¼	teaspoon cumin
¼	teaspoon oregano

Salt and pepper to taste

Heat olive oil in a large cast-iron skillet, add meat, and brown. Add onions, garlic, tomatoes, water, chili powder, cumin, oregano, salt, and pepper, stir well, and simmer for three hours. For thickening, mix a paste consisting of two tablespoons olive oil and two tablespoons flour in a small saucepan, brown slightly, add one cup of water, and stir. Add to chili fifteen minutes before serving, stirring often.

The late Hallie Stillwell is the author of *I'll Gather My Geese*, a wonderful book about her life in the Big Bend region along the Texas-Mexico border. Stillwell had been a schoolteacher, a justice of the peace, rancher, and a newspaper reporter and columnist.

Frank X. Tolbert's Bowl Of Red
Frank X. Tolbert

Adapted *from his groundbreaking book* A Bowl of Red, *this chili recipe has become a standard for many chiliheads.*

12 dried Ancho chile peppers, stemmed and seeded

3 pounds lean beef, trimmed and cubed

3 tablespoon cooking oil (or, if you like your chili a bit greasy like Tolbert's, use a couple ounces of beef suet)

1 tablespoon cumin

1 tablespoon oregano

1 tablespoon cayenne

1 tablespoon Tabasco sauce

2 garlic cloves, minced

1 tablespoon salt

2 tablespoons masa harina

Simmer anchos in a pot of water for one-half hour, remove, place in blender, and puree. Save the liquid and add some to the blender if necessary. Place puree in large cooking pot. In a cast-iron skillet, heat oil (or suet) and brown beef. When done, place beef in cooking pot with puree and add enough of the liquid to cover meat. Bring to boil, reduce heat, and simmer for one-half hour. Add cumin, oregano, cayenne, Tabasco sauce, garlic, and salt, stir, and cook for another forty-five minutes. If you desire a thinner chile, add more of the liquid. If you like thick chili, add masa harina. Cook for additional forty-five minutes, adjusting for taste.

Bob Wiseman's Bowl O' Red
Bob Wiseman

Wiseman, a long-standing competitive chili cook and cookbook author has worn out six Coleman stoves at hundreds of cook-offs. When it comes to whippin' up a bowl o' red, he says, he can "run with the big dogs."

1	tablespoon canola oil
3	pounds sirloin tip roast, trimmed of fat, and cut into 1/4" cubes
2	tablespoons mild chile powder
2	tablespoons paprika
3	tablespoons Gebhardt chili powder
1	tablespoon hot New Mexico chile powder
3	tablespoons cumin
½	teaspoon Mexican oregano
1	cup onion, minced
5	garlic cloves, minced
3	cups chicken stock
1	cup beef stock
2	teaspoons Tabasco
¼	teaspoon cayenne
½	teaspoon sea salt
¼	cup cola-flavored beverage
2	tablespoons fresh lime juice

Heat oil in bottom of Dutch oven, add meat, and cook, turning often, until all of the red is cooked away. Drain. Add the mild chile powder, paprika, Gebhardt chili powder, hot New Mexico chile powder, 2 tablespoons of cumin, oregano, onion, and garlic. Mix until meat is well coated. Add chicken and beef stock, cover, and simmer for two hours. If you prefer a thinner chili, add more chicken stock. Add remaining cumin, hot sauce, cayenne, sea salt, cola beverage, and lime juice. Cover and simmer for another thirty minutes.

Serve with sourdough bread or fresh tortillas and extremely cold beer.

Bob Wiseman is the author of *Healthy Southwestern Cooking* and *Buckskin, Bullets, and Beans*. Hundreds of his recipes have been published in magazines and journals.

Index of Recipes

Other top sellers from Republic of Texas Press

Making it Easy: Cajun Cooking

Chef Arlene Coco

In her mother's kitchen in Baton Rouge, Chef Arlene Coco learned to cook Cajun. Now the secrets of a longtime Louisiana chef are revealed, and among the recipes are family stories of a time when life on the bayou was sweet and simple. The book follows the format of our *Making it Easy* series, simplifying directions for clear understanding and fast, easy preparation, and is divided into several sections, from simple everyday meals to more elaborate menus for entertaining. Each chapter ends with a grocery list for each recipe.

288 pages • 9¼ x 7½ • softbound • ISBN 1-55622-649-7 • $18.95

Top Texas Chefs Cook at Home: Favorite Entrees

Ginnie Siena Bivona

Top Texas Chefs Cook at Home: Favorite Entrees showcases the favorite home cooking recipes of some of the most talented chefs in the state. Each chapter features a story about the chef, his or her life outside the restaurant, hobbies and interests, as well as favorite recipes they use for entertaining in their own homes. The recipes are carefully chosen for simplicity and ease of preparation. Directions are clear and concise, and there is a detailed grocery list, itemized by recipe, for each menu.

244 pages • 9¼ x 7½ • softbound • ISBN 1-55622-651-9 • $18.95

 Visit our web site at **www.wordware.com**

1-55622-648-9 • $15.95

1-55622-537-7 • $16.95

1-55622-569-5 • $18.95

1-55622-613-6 • $16.95

1-55622-575-X • $14.95

1-55622-624-1 • $18.95

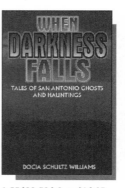

1-55622-536-9 • $16.95

1-55622-377-3 • $16.95

1-55622-571-7 • $18.95